A View From The Centre

The Policing of the National Union of Mineworkers' Dispute 1984 – 1985

David E. Leach

First edition © David E. Leach 2024

The right of David E. Leach to be identified as the author of this work has been asserted in accordance with the Copyright, Designs & Patents Act 1988.

All rights reserved. No part of this book may be reprinted or reproduced or utilised in any form or by any electronic, mechanical or other means, now known or hereafter invented, including photocopying and recording, or in any information storage or retrieval system, without the prior permission in writing of the publishers.

All images are reproduced by permission of South Yorkshire Police, except the images of the author which are owned by him. All copyrights reserved.

Published in Nottingham by Thin Blue Line Books

ISBN 978-1-0685268-0-0

About the author

David Edward Leach BSc joined the Somersetshire Constabulary in 1965. He served in borough and rural stations as well as two postings to road traffic policing centres. In this time he saw service in all of the Western and Central areas of the old county. Following a year at the Police Staff College, Bramshill, in 1973/74, he was a sergeant at Bridgwater and Inspector at headquarters traffic department before secondment to the University of Bristol to gain a degree in Sociology. On his return, he had been at Central police station in Bristol for nine months when the first of the inner-city riots occurred, on 2nd April 1980, during his shift.

In 1983 he was attached to the forward planning unit, under the public order sub-committee of the Association of Chief Police Officers (ACPO), researching tactics and equipment for deployment in large scale public disorder. With only a few weeks of the attachment left to complete, he moved into the National Reporting Centre from its activation for the National Union of Mineworkers dispute. He was to remain there throughout the ensuing year, performing the role of a staff officer to the president of ACPO. He was promoted to chief inspector while carrying out these duties. Following the end of the dispute, he was further attached to ACPO to coordinate the reports of the debrief groups set up to review the policing arrangements.

Upon return to force duties in September 1985, he was the force logistics officer, then a rural sub-divisional commander before being promoted superintendent to take charge of the communications operations department. In this final stage of his police career, he led the process of converting the communications provision of the force into area controls and was part of the national working party which led to the 'Airwave' generation of police hand-held radios.

Upon retirement from the police in 1996, he spent eight years as a communications management consultant in the public safety arena before taking full retirement to spend much of his time working for the National Association of Retired Police Officers (NARPO).

The author at the NRC

Contents

Foreword ii

Introduction iii

1. Historical Perspectives 1
2. National Reporting Centre Operation 11
3. First Few Days 17
4. Accommodating the Demands 26
5. The Operational Demands 47
6. Social and Economic Implications 62
7. Legal Consequences 75
8. Summary 78

Appendix 1 – Chronology of Events 83

Appendix 2 – Collieries 90

Appendix 3 – NRC Floor Plan 94

Appendix 5A – Arrests by Police Force Area 100

Appendix 5B – Arrests by Occupation 102

Appendix 5C – Charges Proffered 105

Appendix 5D – Court Results 108

Appendix 6A – Complaints by Police Force 110

Appendix 6B – Complaints Against Police by Allegation Type . 113

Appendix 7 – Chronology of Intimidation and Violence 114

Index 153

Foreword

In 1983 I was sitting comfortably in my palatial office in Surrey Constabulary headquarters in Guildford, when I was asked to attend the National Reporting Centre at New Scotland Yard to assist the president of ACPO in providing the police response to the ongoing miner's strike. I was aware that getting together the necessary officers from around the country to respond to a wide variety of potential threats was an extremely difficult job logistically, but at that time I did not understand just how difficult.

I was comforted by the police service's ability, proved over the years, to deal with change; but slightly concerned that we may have come to a bridge too far in handling these complex logistical issues. It soon became apparent that the qualities of the officers and others seconded to the NRC were up to the challenge. Their dedication, flexibility and solid experience proved up to the difficult job they had been given to do.

In his thorough, intelligent, and perceptive analysis of this exceptional period for the service, David Leach has dealt with its social, political, and policing aspects in a very influential, insightful, and readable way. It will form a useful and valuable tool for any student of modern social or policing history.

Sir John Smith QPM

Former Deputy Commissioner, Metropolitan Police Service

The author apologises to Sir John Smith, and his family, that there has been a considerable delay in bringing this book to print, brought about by a combination of factors impacting the author. Despite significant effort to renew contact with Sir John, to the date of going to print this has not been successful. Nevertheless, the author feels that Sir John's contribution, through his volunteered Foreword, adds considerably to the work and it has, therefore, been retained.

A View from the Centre

Introduction

It is important to identify at the outset that this book is not intended to be a definitive history of the entire policing arrangements for the National Union of Mineworkers (NUM) Dispute,[1] which lasted from 12th March 1984 until 8th March, 1985. Such a work would require research within and input from almost all of the forty-three current police forces in England and Wales and a separate body of research within Scotland. It is, rather, a detailed report on the perspective on that policing task within England and Wales from the National Reporting Centre (NRC), set down after the passage of many years; and with the greater capacity for objectivity that such a time separation allows. Full details on the role and purpose of the NRC will be outlined in chapter 1.

Time will not have impacted on the accuracy of the information within this document, for that is drawn from notes made by the author during or soon after the events, but the objectivity of the distance in time will, hopefully, make those assessments that are attempted somewhat more objective than may have applied immediately at or after the events.

The author was engaged in the NRC for most of the fifty-one weeks of the 1984 – 85 NUM Dispute and occupied a unique

---

[1] Throughout the work the NUM Miner's Dispute will be primarily referred to as just 'the Dispute', with a capital 'D'.

Introduction

position in respect of what has to be viewed as, by far, the largest policing operation that this country – and possibly the modern Western world – has ever witnessed. Circumstances brought the author and his colleague, for the ten busiest months of the activation of the NRC, to a position unlikely to be repeated; even should such a long operational requirement for the NRC (more recently known as the Mutual Aid Coordination Centre – MACC; and currently the National Police Coordination Centre - NPoCC) again occur. Technology, tactics, operational police planning and approaches have moved on significantly in the forty years hence.

From the twentieth anniversary year there has been some periodic media interest in the aftermath of the NUM Dispute. Most of those who have commented since 2004/5, have chosen to do so from the viewpoint that the significant demise of the coal mining industry in the United Kingdom was a consequence of the government and police activity in 1984 – 85. It is the author's view however, that the response of the government was made appropriate, even unavoidable, by the naked intention of certain individuals and small groups, in and close to the trades' union movement: to use the power of their membership numbers to fatally damage the government of that time This was dependent upon individual union members accepting the lead that was offered and, particularly applicable within the NUM, this willingness was constantly reinforced by peer pressures.

The NUM was the trade union which had been quite successful in this elected government toppling effort, a decade earlier. It was perhaps more valid to perceive elements of the trade union movement at this time as an alternative arm of politics in this country, reaching their most impacting period through the winter of 1978 – 79. It seemed, through 2004/5, that many commentators on the early 1980s had chosen to have selective memories regarding the impact of trades' union activities upon a whole range of this country's manufacturing and commercial interests, and the utilisation of its natural resources through the 1970s.

Within a democratic national political structure, no elected government can, nor should, find itself under the level of threat from any specific interest group as the trades' unions had applied in 1972. For such a situation to prevail is for us all to abandon the democratic structure of governance, whatever its failings, and submit to the edict that selective might is right. After nearly a decade of governments on both sides of the centre ground of party politics being done more damage by pressure groups than at the ballot box, it should not have been a shock to anyone that, eventually, a government would appear that was unprepared to countenance such undemocratic pressures.

Both the legislative and centrally directive activities of the governments in this country have, over the first years of the twenty-first century, done immense damage to the principles which had been set down for policing when the Metropolitan Police was established in 1829. That blueprint had, with appropriate local changes, been applied in all parts of England and Wales by the late 1850s. This approach can be summarised with the popular phrase 'policing by consent' – the broad consent of the population to act responsibly on its behalf. In 1984, however, those principles, and the widened application of

Introduction

constabulary powers established by Royal Commission and subsequent legislation in 1964, remained intact and the police service throughout the UK still remained distinct from politics – especially party politics.

What was seen, certainly by officers at all levels, as the police role throughout the 1984 – 85 NUM Dispute, was no different than what was their stance in all other aspects of their normal activities. Within the law, it was the mission, and sworn duty, of the police service, to even-handedly seek to ensure that all citizens could go about their lawful business unhindered and unintimidated. It had long been a focus of policing, sometimes leading to the creation of Common Law where no statute was wholly appropriate, to exercise an a-political influence to minimise criminal activity at all levels and, traditionally, to maintain "The Queen's Peace".

It has never been the desire of police officers, of any rank and in any part of the UK, to seek confrontation with the public they are sworn to serve. It does become the lot of the police to confront those, whether individual or groups of any size, who seek to break the law and, more importantly perhaps, intend to disrupt the lawful activities of their fellow citizens. Where the numbers of those seeking to cause disruption are low, normal policing arrangements in each area of the country have, traditionally, usually been adequate. As the numbers escalate, whether by virtue of some unexplained attraction or by virtue of a more organised and orchestrated effort, so local police resources will, inevitably, become strained. The recognition of the occasional need for local force numbers to be reinforced was

A View from the Centre

adequately reflected in the *Police Act 1964*, when it extended constables' powers across the whole of England and Wales, rather than just their own or neighbouring force areas, as had been the case previously.

Although the spectre of a national police force would seem to be less of a problem for current political leaders and many commentators, in 1984 – 85 it was used as an accusation promulgated by elements of the mass-media on many occasions and, often, with the NRC held up as its centre of control. Perhaps a national police service is seen by some in political power as more likely to complete the apparent desire for the centralised political control that measures in recent years have pointed toward. In 1984, the Association of Chief Police Officers (ACPO) more than adequately, except for those not wanting to accept the evidence, countered the accusation by identifying that the coordination by the NRC was wholly in support of those individual forces finding themselves under greater pressure than their normal resources could handle. This provision had made any move away from locally based forces unnecessary - as well as undesirable.

As well as attempting to describe the long series of events through much of 1984 and into the early months of 1985, this document sets out to give a more objective view of what happened over that period than many, thus far, have produced. To those who have some reason to view it as such, it will, of course, be a piece of delayed police propaganda but at least it is based upon the facts as they played out at the time. If it does appear, even to the truly independent reader, to be slanted

Introduction

towards supporting the policing activity through those fifty-one weeks, the author makes no apology. It is, after all, time that a document was available for posterity that gives as full a picture as the author can manage to set some of the records straight. After some of the rather one-sided media presentations at the twentieth, twenty-fifth and thirtieth anniversaries, it is hoped that this document can, albeit belatedly, show a counterbalance.

In this introductory passage, it is vital that the author claims full responsibility for the content of this document. While it is hoped that the mass of current and former police officers at all levels will approve of this effort to relate what happened, none of those referred to in the following pages share responsibility for this report. Although the politics of the twenty-first century in the UK have had a less than beneficial impact upon policing in these countries, the massive policing effort in the mid-1980s must be seen as having, at that time, secured the rule of law and the democratic process when both came under severe threat. It is inevitable that some readers will not share some of the interpretations which the author places upon what was happening throughout this, often tumultuous, year. All the author can ask is that where readers want to find alternative explanations they, at least, recognise that the view that the author espouses was difficult to avoid, given the sustained activity, through rhetoric and activity 'on the ground', which was so often manifested.

If there is need for any dedication for a work such as this document, it should be addressed to all those police officers – leaders and front line – who provided such an effort as seemed impossible before it was achieved and amazing after the events. The politics do not seem to allow for more than a passing 'thank you' from those in the highest positions in the land for police officers engaged in such an important campaign to prevent large-scale breaches of the law. During the street disorders that preceded and followed the 1984 – 85 NUM Dispute, as well as during that year, there were many individual acts of heroism by police officers and many instances of strong leadership, initiative and organisational skills, some of them leaving those outside the service astounded at their achievement. None were recognised by the types of awards, even campaign medals, which would, undoubtedly, have followed any military operation of even lesser scale.

In the most recent past decade or so, a whole new perspective relating to the traditional, deep mine and open cast, production of coal has developed. This relates to the contribution towards the, variously identified, pollution of the Earth's atmosphere contributed to the use of fossil fuels.

The author wishes to place on record my sincere thanks to all those officers and staff with whom he was associated throughout 1984/85. He also owes a considerable debt of thanks to Tom Andrews for his careful reading of the draft for this book, for his assistance in making it better than it would, otherwise, have been and, of course, for his facilitating its publication. Not least, I thank Sir John Smith for his generous comments in his *Foreword*.

Introduction

The author would also like to take the personal opportunity to publicly thank his late wife and three, at the time of the NUM Dispute, very young, daughters for their unswerving support in what was, for them, a year with precious little support from him.

A View from the Centre

1. Historical Perspectives

<u>The Political & Union Perspective</u>

The activities of various trades' unions through the 1970s are without the remit of this paper but are very much part of the background to the events which happened between 1983 and 1985. The collective memory of the recent history of this time, was of the actions of trades' union members forcing immense consequences upon the whole country. Governments of both ends of the party-political spectrum had experienced the impact, and it is without much doubt that the inability to deal effectively with such activity had led to the electorate seeking changes of government. By way of example, those who are old enough to remember the 1970s will clearly recall the reduced working week, and having to keep a good stock of candles.

Dubbed by the mass-media as the "Winter of Discontent", these pressures had been at their most severe and widest impact during the period from the Autumn of 1978 until run-up to the general election of May 1979. The electorate appeared to have had enough and were, as they had earlier in the 1970s, seeking a new government to meet the challenge. That this had not been the result earlier in the decade did not matter, the majority of the voting population were, perhaps in some desperation, seeking another change. In the preceding four years, the only female party-political leader had been seen as someone who was prepared to deal with issues, and subsequently Margaret

Thatcher became the first female British Prime Minister in May 1979.

While the leadership of several large trades' unions had demonstrated their desire to impose their minority group views on governments of whatever political persuasion through the 1970s, the Conservative government from 1979 was seen as a most legitimate target for such actions. In the first years following the 1979 election, there had been other matters for the police to confront and for the government to focus upon as the key concern. On 2nd April 1980, following a relatively low-key (by modern standards) raid on an illegal drinking establishment believed to be an outlet for drug dealing, street rioting occurred in the St Paul's area of Bristol on a scale not seen for a long time. Although many observers, including chief police officers in other parts of the country, saw the St Paul's rioting as an isolated incident, they were to be proved woefully wrong in the April and July of 1981, when several large conurbations saw young people taking to the streets in large numbers. This was most noticeable in Brixton, London; and Toxteth, Liverpool; but similar rioting spread through Birmingham, Manchester and Leeds.

Following these widespread and violent disturbances, the whole country saw a cause for concern. After all, the previous disturbances that people could remember at that time, all had a focus, such as 'Ban The Bomb', or the American involvement in Vietnam. The street disturbances of the very early 1980s were seen as being not directed at achieving anything in particular, but were more intended to disable the rule of law. Much anguish was to be expressed, thereafter, about deprivation and seeking to understand the young and minority groups. The legacy of much of that effort, almost an industry, can be perceived as being far less to bring such groups into the mainstream of social intercourse than to isolate individuals and make our society less cohesive. In the attempt to meet the perceived need to 'understand', often defined by those with no first-hand experience, there has developed a state philosophy to placate rather than bring into line those who want to pursue their own way, regardless of its impact on others. We should, perhaps, not be surprised at the outcome of such an approach as it has been manifested over the early years of the twenty-first century.

1982 brought a pressure on the government of a very different nature, when the Argentine government decided to invade the Falkland Islands. Alongside all this, of course, the situation in Northern Ireland and the ongoing terrorism associated with Irish Republicanism continued to be the threat to mainland security, that had been too often and dramatically demonstrated throughout the 1970s.

Following the Bristol St Paul's riots in 1980, chief constables varied greatly in their recognition as to whether those pressures could ever come their way. Preparation, in both officer training, and equipment acquisition, was extremely uneven, to the point of being haphazard. The policing response to riots in 1981 demonstrated beyond doubt the lacklustre state of policing equipment for dealing with such situations.

The aftermath of the multi-centred street disturbances of 1981 changed that situation, with ACPO taking the initiative to prepare that all forces should be ready to confront such large-scale situations – whether in their own territory or providing assistance to other forces. Key to this effort was the proper training of officers in confronting such a scale of disorder, including in 1981 the use of contrived petrol bombs in some areas, and equipping officers with both protective clothing and protected vehicles. Centrally, ACPO established the Public Order Sub-Committee, under the long-established General Purposes Committee of the association, and, in liaison with the commissioner of the Metropolitan Police, supported that sub-committee with a team of officers at New Scotland Yard (NSY), known as the Public Order Forward Planning Unit (POFPU). The initial task was to produce notes of guidance, known as the *Tactical Options Manual*, and then to establish the detailed manoeuvres within such tactics and to test and evaluate appropriate items of equipment for use in public disorder situations.

Police Mutual Aid Arrangements

The foundations of the British police services followed on, falteringly, over a period of nearly thirty years from the establishment of the Metropolitan Police in 1829. Some areas had seen the setting up of city and borough forces, enabled by the *Municipal Corporations Act 1836*, but they were usually quite numerically small. Reaction to the *County Police Act 1839*, which went no further than 'permitting' the setting up of forces, was not overwhelming. In many, predominantly rural, areas the long-established system of parish constables in support of local Justices of the Peace (magistrates) had proven to be adequate. Local citizens elected to serve in a law enforcement capacity by their peers, or paying 'substitutes' to do so, aligned strongly with the historic British principle of collective responsibility. Such persons knew the residents of their parish, and outsiders faced a widespread mistrust, and thus the parish constable system – at least in rural areas – generally sufficed. It was not until the *County & Borough Police Act 1856* that it was mandated from central government that police forces must be established in all areas – twenty-seven years after such arrangements were found to be effective in London.

By 1860 each county and a multitude of cities and boroughs had appointed constables and senior officers. Outside London and the significantly larger cities however, individual establishments were not huge, but the number of forces was considerable. The most credible source has identified over 500 forces that have existed in Britain since 1829.[2] In such circumstances it was an early development that chief constables should call upon their colleagues for assistance, but this was, in an era of still only developing mobility and communications, predominantly on a localised basis. Before the *Police Act 1964*, the powers of constables were applicable only in their own, appointed, areas and in neighbouring counties or in boroughs within their county. This was all that was required until the arrival of greater mobility which developed after World War II.

---

[2] Stallion, Martin and Wall, David (2011) *The British Police: Forces and Chief Officers 1829 – 2012* Hook: The Police History Society

Historical Perspectives

In the 1964 Act, the powers of constables in England & Wales were extended to cover the whole of the two countries. There had, earlier, been longer distanced examples of aid from other forces, such as support to Glamorganshire for disturbances in the mining valleys of South Wales in 1911, but in each case the incoming officers had to be sworn-in locally for them to be fully deployable by the resident chief constable: which still to this day is the case for English and Welsh officers on mutual aid to Scotland.

All of the smaller separate urban forces were subsumed into their surrounding counties by the late 1960s, most around the years either side of World War II, although quite a few resisted for as long as they were able. By the late 1960s many city and borough forces were compelled to become part of their surrounding county forces with most doing so in 1968. Not until the consequence for policing structure that accompanied the wide scale change to local government boundaries in 1974 had the point been reached that still prevailed in 1984 (and today), with forty-three police forces in England & Wales and, until 2013 with the creation of the single Police Scotland, a further nine north of the border. Following the changes in 1974, with the sole exception of the City of London Police, forces were of a more significant size in all areas, with the smallest around 1,000 in establishment. Hence the capacity for chief constables to deal with quite large situations without recourse to calling for assistance from other force areas, was reasonably assured.

The industrial unrest of the 1970s and street disorders of the early 1980s were, of course, exceptional and many instances can be recorded of police officers travelling to other parts of the country to support colleagues under pressures that those 'home' forces could not meet alone. From the first significant strenuous picketing in 1972, it became evident to ACPO that there was an occasional need for the mutual aid arrangements to be centrally coordinated. Not to have done so was certain to result in aid being sought by more than one force at a time and the responses of the forces providing the assistance becoming confused. In conjunction with the ACPO planning for the NRC, a mutual aid provision capability formula was agreed and set at one police support unit (PSU) – then 1 inspector, 2 sergeants & 20 constables – per 200 of each force's establishment – equating to roughly ten percent of each force being suitably trained and equipped.

The National Reporting Centre

After much discussion within ACPO and with government ministers, an embryonic National Reporting Centre facility was established. It was to be under the direct control of the current president of ACPO, chosen at that time by his (there were no female chief constables until the 1990s) peers and serving for one year from each September ACPO conference. ACPO had a small suite of permanent offices in New Scotland Yard and the NRC was to be housed, when required, in that building, with the Metropolitan Police providing both space and personnel to operate the facility.

Historical Perspectives

The structure and staffing of the NRC from March 1984 is to be covered in the next chapter but it is worth pointing out at this stage that the centre had remained dormant for most of the time since its conception. Activations were very few and were never for long periods. Its inception had recognised that it may need only to monitor events and most commonly in its previous activations, that is all it had done. That the 1984 NUM Dispute would be extended over such a long period of time and be multi-centred could not have been realistically anticipated, even in the early days of that dispute. Even the numbers for mutual aid determined in the 1970s would prove not to meet the needs of this activation.

It is worthwhile, to put the 1984 – 85 activation of the NRC into perspective, to identify that the following were the only activations since its inception and Home Office approval in 1973:

From	To	Event
10th February 1974	7th March 1974	NUM Dispute
21st October 1980	28th February 1981	Prison officers' dispute
6th July 1981	31st August 1981	Street disorders
27th May 1982	1st June 1982	Papal visit

During the prison officers' dispute the principal activity within the NRC had been the allocation of prisoners to be housed in police stations throughout the country, as Her Majesty's Prisons were only accepting very limited numbers of those remanded or sentenced from the courts. In all other activations, the NRC had gone no further than monitoring the local mutual aid arrangements and did not reach a point at which centralised allocations became necessary.

The build-up to the NUM Dispute 1984

The early 1980s saw the introduction of legislation designed to curb the power of trade union leaders, through requirements for union members to be balloted before strike action could be exercised. Although the strike and other actions by the NUM through the 1970s had caused or contributed alongside the activities of other unions, severe impact upon the wider population, it had not, evidently, been the success that the union desired. In the Autumn of 1983, with every appearance that the Conservative government was well established and seeking to rationalise the public purse subsidy to the coal mining industry, the NUM declared an overtime ban to apply pressure to the National Coal Board. With the Winter of 1983 – 84 seeing no tangible product from the overtime ban, by the Spring of 1984 it was looking very much as though the NUM would move to strike action.

Over the weekend of 10th/11th March 1984, it became apparent that the NUM leadership was heading towards imminent strike action. With no national ballot, there was also a strong potential that there would be a differential response to the leadership's move and a likely effort to impose strike actions in coalfield areas content to remain only with the overtime ban.

Historical Perspectives

The experiences in the 1970s proved that if this scenario materialised, activities beyond peaceful picketing could be expected and ACPO realised the need to urgently plan for such an eventuality.

Probably the most earnest wish to remain only with an overtime ban rested in the Nottinghamshire coalfield area, with other coalfield areas in relatively close proximity, deciding to follow the NUM leadership call to move toward strike action. This was perceived, correctly, to have the greatest potential for a development beyond peaceful picketing and attention by striking miners from areas outside of Nottinghamshire. The first days of the move to strike action will be dealt with in chapter three.

For its ease of reference, the chronology of some of the significant events through the NUM Dispute, as reported by the mass-media, are contained in appendix 1. At this distance in time, it seems quite significant that, after the initial impact, much of the day-to-day activity at collieries and most of that, perhaps more sinister, in colliery communities, attracted relatively little mass-media attention. To further set the scene, a list of collieries as existed before the commencement of the strike action is reproduced at appendix 2.

2. National Reporting Centre Operation

The plan for the layout and facilities of the National Reporting Centre had been revised by a report into the operation of the NRC in 1981. This had followed the activation for the multi-centre street disorders of the April of that year and proved adequate for the same circumstance in that July. On both occasions it had not gone beyond monitoring mutual aid arrangements. That plan proved to be robust enough for the initial stages of the 1984 activation and, although the deployment board content was changed considerably to record the current residential deployments, the layout of the room remained physically much the same throughout the NUM dispute activation. A schematic plan of the main room of the NRC, as it was after the first few days in March 1984, is reproduced at appendix 3 and will, hopefully, help to contextualise the description in this chapter.

On the thirteenth floor of the main block of New Scotland Yard, on the side overlooking the main entrance off Broadway, were two meeting rooms divided by a folding partition. With this partition open, one large room was created. The construction of the (then new) NSY in the 1960s was modular on most upper floors, enabling rooms of varied size to be created by more substantial partition walls. Alongside the main room was a single window store room in which were kept all the whiteboards for

National Reporting Centre operation

display of various aspects of resources and deployments. Although consideration had been given to the NRC sharing the established facility elsewhere in NSY for casualty bureau operation, this was wisely dismissed as an option as there was some potential for a casualty bureau to be required to run simultaneous with a NRC activation. Hence there was a connectivity provision for telephony services in the combined meeting rooms that would not have been required for their everyday use and which awaited an NRC activation. In the first day of the 1984 activation, it was realised that the senior officers would need a room separate from the main room and an office just beyond the storeroom was committed to this purpose.

The telephony communications were in the form of multi-key instruments with all lines being accessible from each instrument. Although they provided a facility for 'internal' calls between instruments, the relatively close proximity of all personnel made this unnecessary and it was only used to transfer incoming calls between instruments. Although the telex facilities which were housed elsewhere in NSY were employed, much use was made of the messaging facility of the Police National Computer (PNC) which was capable of being accessed through a terminal positioned in the NRC.

With the NRC normally dormant, not even instantly available, there were two levels of activation which were notified to forces through messages 'broadcast' via the PNC at the direction of the president of ACPO. Although the arrangements initiated in the 1970s and revisited in 1981 had housed the NRC in New Scotland Yard, it had been agreed by ACPO council that the incumbent president should be responsible for the operation of the centre. ACPO council was the full assembly of all forty-one chief constables in England and Wales and the two commissioners (Metropolitan and City of London Police). The totality of ACPO membership includes all chief officer ranks, in other words all officers above the rank of chief superintendent. Although not the case since around the turn of this century, in the 1980s the president was elected by his peers from among the members of ACPO council and served for one year in that post from the ACPO conference held in each September. The allocating of responsibility for any NRC activation to the current president was intended to mitigate any view that the Metropolitan Police, by far the largest force in the country, was in any way directing the activities of other forces.

The incumbent president from September 1983 had been the chief constable of the Humberside Police, David Hall. Perhaps with some degree of good fortune, he was also the chairman of the ACPO general purposes committee, which held responsibility for public order matters. He and his ACPO council colleagues, especially those within whose areas collieries were situated, had been closely watching developments since the invoking of the overtime ban by the NUM shortly after his election.

Over the weekend of 10th/11th March 1984, the NUM executive determined, without complying with the legal requirement to hold a ballot of the wider membership, that there should be an escalation to strike action. It was recognised from the outset, indeed had been anticipated for some months, that the response of miners could be less than totally supportive of the NUM leadership decision should they act in this non-consultative manner. Reactions to the call for strike action proved this to be the case and, most significantly, the miners in the Nottinghamshire coalfield area collectively determined to continue with the overtime ban but not to move to strike action.

Anticipating that such a differential response on the part of miners in some areas would lead to the NUM seeking to enforce their diktat through unwelcome picketing activity, and that this could result in confrontation, the ACPO president consulted with senior colleagues and Home Office officials on Tuesday 13th March 1984. As these moves were being made in London, the fears of the ACPO officers were realised when there was disorderly confrontation between miners seeking to enter collieries in Nottinghamshire and pickets who were almost all from outside that area. The situation in Nottinghamshire demanded that the Chief Constable there, Charles MacLachlan, had to commit not only a large proportion of his own manpower resources to the problem, but also seek mutual aid, in the form of 14 PSUs (182 officers), from neighbouring forces.

Consequently, it was decided by the president of ACPO that the NRC should be opened and that it should assume its monitoring status from 07:00 hours on Wednesday 14th March 1984. To further reinforce the fact that the NRC was not being controlled by the Metropolitan Police, and in the light of his own staff officer needing to be committed to his direct assistance, the president sought other non-Metropolitan Police officers to fill the role of his staff officers in the NRC. At the suggestion of the general secretary of ACPO, a retired assistant chief constable who was accommodated in the offices in NSY, the president visited the Public Order Forward Planning Unit (POFPU) and requested of the chief superintendent overseeing it, that officers from that unit from provincial forces be made available to fill this role.

All officers were members of the POFPU by virtue of their previous experience in dealing with public order issues. One was a superintendent from the South Wales Constabulary, who had joined the unit earlier that year from the post of task force commander in his force and who, incidentally, came from a mining family. The other was an inspector from the Avon and Somerset Constabulary (the author), who had been closely involved in the riot in Bristol in 1980 and with the arrangements in that force to meet any repetition of that situation. With the president and his in-force staff officer, these officers were present on the command side of the NRC from early on the morning of 14th March 1984.

The bulk of the staff on the controller side of the NRC on 14th March were drawn from the courts administration department of the Metropolitan Police. One aspect established from the outset and that stood the test of time was that the control staff was provided in twelve-hours shifts: the 'day' personnel working from 0700 hours to 1900 hours and a smaller contingent covering the night shift. The senior Metropolitan officer on day shifts was a chief superintendent, supported by five others of various ranks with a chief inspector, supported by two others, on night shifts and both day and night shifts at

National Reporting Centre operation

weekends. Included in the initial day shifts was a Metropolitan inspector who became the only officer, other than the provincial officers, to remain at the NRC throughout this activation.

The arrangements within the NRC, although they had been planned well and were basically sound, had to undergo detail modifications quite rapidly in the first days and weeks of the 1984 – 85 activation. These changes will be dealt with later, as the story of the activation is revealed. The remainder of this book will follow a relatively chronological format and the changes demanded will be dealt with as they arose.

3. First Few Days

As has already been outlined, the first day of strenuous activity by striking miners against those wishing to go to work in the Nottinghamshire coalfield, Tuesday 13th March 1984, had resulted in the deployment of police officers from all parts of the Nottinghamshire force area and had required that Chief Constable MacLachlan seek aid from his neighbouring forces. That day a total of fourteen PSUs had been deployed by surrounding forces into the Nottinghamshire area, in support of local officers. It has to be said that by the previous standards this was, itself, a significant level of mutual aid; but such numbers were to pale in the light of what was to be provided from the following day.

All forces had been pre-warned and were officially notified of the activation of the NRC from 0700 hours on the morning of Wednesday 14th March 1984, with the indication that the centre was at 'monitoring only' status. This meant that forces could make individual requests to their neighbouring forces for assistance but had to notify the NRC of any such deployments.

There was much activity within the NRC as officers in the controller's team made contact with all forces to establish their preparedness to allocate PSUs should they be required and, perhaps of even greater importance, to attempt to identify which forces perceived that they may have a need to call for assistance. The picture was relatively calm throughout all but the

First Few Days

Nottinghamshire coalfield area, with almost all other miners having accepted, albeit sometimes grudgingly, the NUM leadership's direction to commence strike action.

From this early stage it was recognised that the information flow from all areas required coordination, as much as did the availability and potential deployment of officers. This was really the start point for an important, information gathering and dissemination, role within the NRC. A Metropolitan Police inspector was allocated this role at that early stage and he was the same one who remained in the Centre throughout the activation.

The opening of the NRC proved to be of interest to both the senior officers within the Metropolitan Police and senior officials from within the Home Office, and several visited the centre during that morning. At 1145 hours, a telephone call was received from the control room of the Nottinghamshire Constabulary and was picked up by the superintendent from South Wales (NRC staff officer). His first reaction to the call was to identify that he had better write down what was being requested! With a large influx of striking miners assembling to confront the miners wishing to continue to go to work, the chief constable of Nottinghamshire had realised that the only safe reaction was to present large enough numbers of police officers to try to deter any repetition of the Violences encountered twenty-four hours earlier.

The request from Nottinghamshire was for a staggering fifty PSUs – some 1,150 officers – to be at the Nottinghamshire

A View from the Centre

Police Headquarters, Sherwood Lodge, just north of the city of Nottingham, by 1600 hours that day. The request recognised that the single deployment of large numbers of police officers would not bring a close of the matter and there were further requests for groups of sixty-five PSUs at 0400 hours and 1200 hours over each of the following two days. The president of ACPO, with several senior police officers and Home Office officials was in the NRC at the time that the call was received and, having been acquainted with the numbers being asked for, he took the officials out of the room, with the direction that his newly appointed staff officers get on with the job in hand. All forces in England and Wales were notified, by a Police National Computer broadcast, that the NRC was moving from 'monitoring' to 'active' status; which meant that all forces seeking assistance must, from that point in time, make their applications to the NRC for the Centre to request the aid, maintaining an overall picture of demand and supply.

The morning's telephone contact with forces paid off admirably and the Metropolitan Police officers on the controller's side of the NRC set about contacting the forces as indicated by the staff officers. The usual way in which a PSU was transported was in two personnel carriers, and the frenetic activity both in the NRC and the various forces close enough to Nottingham brought forty-nine-and-a-half PSUs to Sherwood Lodge by 1600 hours. The remaining personnel carrier, from the Norfolk Constabulary, suffered a puncture on the journey and arrived at 1615 hours. The deployment of 1,150 officers on mutual aid in a little over four hours from the initial call for the assistance was, of itself, a resounding reflection of the planning since 1981, and a result of the considerable effort and will to succeed of a great many police officers.

The necessary arrangements were made, in a slightly more relaxed fashion, for the further numbers of PSUs to be sent to Nottinghamshire for the following two days. It may have been fortunate, in that initial concentration of activity within the NRC and far beyond in the many forces contacted, that only Nottinghamshire sought assistance in that first week. This enabled the staff, on both the command, and control sides of the NRC and those officers in force operations rooms across the country, to get into a method of working which would, quite soon, have to be capable of meeting far more complex deployment demands.

While the initial fifty PSUs were being assembled and deployed to Nottinghamshire's Sherwood Lodge, there was need for frequent contact with the Nottinghamshire operations room (force control room). This proved, very soon, to be less than adequate as the level of activity at Sherwood Lodge too often meant that all manned telephone lines were already in use. The superintendent staff officer sought the assistance of the POFPU staff, and a Metropolitan Police inspector was dispatched to Sherwood Lodge to act as liaison. He made the journey in good time and established himself on a telephone line near the operations room to provide a ready means of communication between Nottinghamshire and the NRC. His commitment to this task was soon made unnecessary by the rapid development of structures at Sherwood Lodge, but it proved to be invaluable in that early rush of activity.

A View from the Centre

From the first day, it was evident that there was considerable interest from within the government in what was taking place, but the president and his senior ACPO colleagues, not least the chief constable of Nottinghamshire, sought to ensure that there was no evidence of any political interference with the operational policing role. At that time, but a position dramatically eroded during more recent times, the operational autonomy of chief constables was still, and rightly, seen as a vital element in the checks and balances of our democratic structure. Indeed, writing only a few years previously in 1978, Her Majesty's Chief Inspector of Constabulary Eric St Johnstone had stated, "it has been said that in operational matters a chief constable is answerable to God, his Queen, his conscience, and to no one else.".[3]

The demand for information was such that the president instructed his newly acquired staff officers, on the morning of Thursday 15th March 1984, to prepare a report on the activity of the previous day. This report by the staff officers to the president became a daily feature from that day and throughout the activation. These reports were, in those first days, typed and copied by the staff officers, more than once assisted by the president himself, and presented before 0900 hours each day. The president allowed for a copy of this report to be handed to a senior Home Office official, usually an assistant under-secretary, who called at the NRC each morning for a briefing by the staff

---

[3] St Johnston, Eric (1978) *One Policeman's Story* Chichester: Barry Rose p. 153

officers and then attended a meeting with his Energy Ministry counterparts.

The deployment of such significant numbers of police officers in the Nottinghamshire coalfield area had a real and beneficial preventative impact upon the levels of violence that may otherwise have been seen. There was plenty enough intimidation on offer to those miners wanting to do their routine shifts, but few were denied access to their collieries. In most colliery areas, Nottinghamshire included, the working week commenced with a 'wind-down' of miners into the pit on Sunday evening and ended with the lunch-time wind down on a Friday. The departure of miners at the end of their Friday shift seldom realised much in the way of picketing activity. As a precaution and to enable some respite for his local officers, Chief Constable MacLachlan of Nottinghamshire requested, and received, twenty-five PSUs overnight on both Friday 16th and Saturday 17th March.

It was anticipated, correctly, that the demands upon the NRC would be much less over the weekend. With no working miners to rail against, no picketing activity was to be seen to be appropriate. Although, the pattern of intimidation within residential mining communities continued unabated over the weekends and produced considerable policing demands at local level. The crew of three Metropolitan Police officers, under the command of a chief inspector were allocated on each of the twelve-hour shifts. Over the first three weekends, with the full extent of what may occur as yet unknown, one of the provincial staff officers remained in London to represent the president of ACPO at the Centre.

From that first week it was evident that the activity within the coalfield areas was going to become both more strenuous and more widespread. Before the end of the first week, several chief constables of forces in mining areas identified that there were miners, in varying numbers, showing early signs that they wanted to attend their collieries to work. The experience in Nottinghamshire through that first week made it plain that each of the forces where miners wanted to go back to work would be subjected to similar picketing pressures. In the last days of that first week five other forces sought assistance for the following Sunday evening wind-down.

The situation in most other areas was somewhat different than that in Nottinghamshire. In the Nottinghamshire coalfield area, the majority of miners wanted to work, albeit maintaining the overtime ban of the previous six months. In most other colliery areas, there were comparatively few miners who were prepared to declare that they did not agree with the direction of the NUM national leadership to move to strike action without holding a ballot. These miners – in some collieries but a single man – were much more open to intimidation and needed quite a large police presence to secure their safety.

It is worthy of identification that the NUM offered no strike pay from union funds, instead deploying their not inconsiderable financial resources to meeting expenses incurred by those of their members willing to take part in picketing activity and to travel to other areas to deter their fellow miners from resisting the dictates from the national leadership.

On the afternoon of Sunday 18th March 1984, a total of 299 PSUs (some 6,877 officers!) were travelling from their home forces, all across the country, to the five forces whose chief constables were seeking to ensure that police numbers were a deterrent to Violences on picket lines. In the first week of the activation, it was realised that the commitment could spread far beyond Nottinghamshire and that the travel involved for forces any distance from those with collieries would become a significant additional time factor for officers in the PSUs. It was therefore arranged (with considerable difficulty relating to local politics in some areas) for the forces making the biggest requests for mutual aid manpower to accommodate officers through the week. All manner of establishments were employed, including military bases, to accommodate officers in 'dormitory' type space, with the additional considerations of feeding and washing facilities.

The five forces that received mutual aid in this fashion for the week commencing on the Sunday night wind-down on 18th March were: Derbyshire, Leicestershire, North Wales, Nottinghamshire, and Warwickshire. This, of itself, demonstrated how quickly the confrontations between working and striking miners in Nottinghamshire were spreading to the other coalfield areas. Also during that week, smaller numbers of PSUs, deployed on a daily basis, were sent to both Staffordshire and Cumbria.

A View from the Centre

These, what turned out to be, early days of a very long activation of the NRC and deployments of significant numbers of officers on mutual aid to other police forces had brought to the fore a whole raft of demands. Although the basic structure within the NRC and the pre-determined arrangements for mutual aid proved to be well-thought-out and robust, this was a situation that demanded some quick thinking at all levels. There was some improvisation but most of the measures adopted, and perhaps later adapted, proved to be resilient as the time passed. The following chapter deals with those, sometimes innovative measures.

4. Accommodating the Demands

The outline commitment of forces to mutual aid, agreed in the 1970s, was one PSU for every 200 of force establishments, with a different formula applicable to the Metropolitan Police. This produced a total theoretical availability in England and Wales of 491 PSUs – 11,293 officers. The abstraction of the PSU commitment of those forces requesting aid from Sunday 18th March 1984 from the national figure presented an equally theoretical potential of 434 PSUs (9,982 officers) being available from the areas which were not being directly affected by miner's pickets. In other words, almost the entire spare national capacity, including officers on rest-days or coming off night shifts and the like. It was furthermore recognised, that some of the forces which had not yet requested mutual aid, could be anticipating activity in their areas which would render it nonsensical to dispatch officers to other parts of the country. The request was therefore issued from the NRC for forces to indicate revised commitments of personnel and to identify what, if any, of those additional PSU numbers would have to be formed of officers who had not been fully trained in confronting large-scale public disorder. The product of the responses of forces to this request was a total of 649 PSUs (14,927 officers).

As considered above, it was soon realised that economies in terms of travelling time could be achieved by accommodating officers in, or close to, the affected areas. The move to accommodating officers, while it made for massive saving in the travelling times which were encountered in the first week, produced a need for the individuals to be afforded some, albeit intermittent 'home time' and a return to family life. The theoretical maximum availability had, therefore, to be viewed in the light that, what became known within the service as, 'residential aid', necessitated individual officers being committed, wherever achievable, no more frequently than on alternate weeks.

It must be remembered that the demands being placed upon officers required that they invariably worked extended tours of duty. The conditions then applicable and laid down under *Police Regulations* provided that, for those up to the rank of chief inspector and while away on aid to other areas, were entitled to overtime payments which equated to eight hours per day. This meant that the senior officers were relieved of the usual consideration for economising on hours worked, as a full additional eight hours' payment was due regardless of actual hours deployed. In most instances, this manifested as both long operational and 'stand-by' deployments for most of the officers who were away from their home forces. It is worthy of mention that those officers remaining within their home forces were often expected to work equally long hours, and with little time for family, even though they were returning to their homes between their shifts.

The Chief Constable of the South Wales Police, David East, had an additional, at least perceived, limitation on any call he may have to make for assistance; although the strike was throughout the summer months to be 'solid' in that area, in that the miners were unanimous in their support for it and thus presenting no police involvement to protect working men. The local recollections, going back to 1911 and repeated in the 1930s, was very negative towards any police officers other than those native to Welsh constabularies. Memories of much earlier confrontations between miners and police officers drafted in from English forces remained bitter, and the chief constable did not want them rekindled.

This presented a potential problem for the NRC, in that all three forces along the southern half of Wales had collieries and both Dyfed Powys and Gwent forces were, in any case, relatively small numerically. Through much of the year, a reserve of available mutual aid was kept back in forces such as Avon and Somerset, Gloucestershire, and Wiltshire, to enable a response across the Severn Bridge should the forces in South Wales encounter a need that would force them to abandon this, Welsh police only, desire. As it played out, the only call for assistance in South Wales was of limited duration, in July, to help confront the attention by striking miners to the lorry convoys attempting to transport imported coal from the docks; after the problem in similar circumstances, had been encountered on the route between Humberside and South Yorkshire.

Although the increased commitments from forces and accommodating of personnel in the most affected areas gave some greater latitude regarding the deployments for each successive week, the personnel in the NRC realised the importance of maximising the utility of the aid. After the (largely precautionary) attention in the first few days, the staff officers committed to arrive at the NRC as early in the morning as the prevailing conditions across the colliery areas demanded. In addition, they were accommodated in London and were called out by the night duty Metropolitan team on a number of occasions. Although the commitment of one of them remaining in London over weekends was only undertaken as a precaution for the first few weeks, the early starts to the day remained a feature for much of the remainder of 1984. The principal operational reason for the early starts, was to maximise the benefits to currently affected areas of the PSUs deployed on residential aid, by allowing for their deployment in preparation for any emerging picketing activity. There was a secondary benefit in that the staff officers, with the assistance of the inspector, information officer, and typist, who arrived at New Scotland Yard by 0700 hours each weekday, were enabled to prepare the daily incident report to the ACPO president by 0900 hours on most mornings.

The availability of manpower to some chief constables was hindered, and even obstructed, by local politicians. In a few cases it was even by impeded by those on their own local police authorities – the civilian oversight board of forces. Where this occurred, it was a strong identification that the political motivation of some councillors was perhaps stronger than their acceptance of their responsibilities to all their electorate. The prevailing ethos of the chief constable being in full operational command of his force mitigated the potential consequences of these localised attempts to impede his ability to provide the protection of the Queen's Peace, which was his primary duty.

Accommodating the Demands

Such independence, particularly from police authority intervention, had fortunately been enshrined in the Royal Commission into the Police in 1962, which had largely been prompted by authority meddling into operational police matters, coincidentally also in Nottingham, and the resultant *Police Act 1964*. While not all chief constables in the affected areas were of the same mind in all respects, they all saw their duty as clearly demanding that in the absence of any potentially unifying NUM ballot in favour of strike action, those choosing to work should, wherever possible, be enabled to do so. This was coupled with the common law responsibility of the police to preserve the Queen's Peace and prevent offences against people or property, which included the miners who wished to work.

Where such political constraints made accommodating the necessary reserves of manpower either impossible or unrealistically restricted, other chief constables came to the support of their potentially disadvantaged ACPO colleague. While the figures contained in appendix 4 are, largely, reflective of the demands being encountered by the relevant forces, some of the mutual aid accommodated was really there in support of those neighbouring forces unable to accommodate it. This facilitated the daily (or sometimes several times within any given day) re-deployments of PSUs across force boundaries to meet the demands currently being encountered. These re-deployments were all made through the NRC and recorded there. As the Dispute progressed and for some time after it had ended, the resort to these records in order for forces to settle their accounts proved to be quite a challenge to the book-keepers.

Each weekday morning, from as early as the prevailing dynamics of the situation demanded, the staff officers would engage in trying to determine what area was to be the 'target of the day' for the massive numbers of roving pickets being assembled by the NUM. By far the most reliable information in this regard came from a somewhat unexpected source.

By 1984, both the BBC and Independent Television News companies had started broadcasting morning programmes, each a mix of news and current affairs, which went out live from 0600 or 0700 hours. From 0500, and during the programmes, the researchers employed in their respective newsrooms started telephoning the NRC for the latest situation reports. During the earlier of these calls there was seldom much of a picture obtained from the colliery area police forces, but the researchers often knew more than the staff officers did. A process had soon been developed by the mass media organisations through which local reporters and cameramen or photographers would be out and about from very early each day. Most of these reporters and photographers worked freelance for the national media, although many were junior reporters on local newspapers, and they were keen to report back to the national daily newspapers, television, and radio London offices, what was going on in their areas. Frequently the first identification within the NRC of a build-up of mobile pickets was through comments received from the BBC and ITN researchers.

Accommodating the Demands

As the picture was developing and with frequent liaison with force control rooms in affected areas, the staff officers would re-deploy the residential mutual aid units on duty from the forces that were accommodating them, into the force which had the greater current need. Although distance of travel had to be considered, it was likely that, with the most affected areas being around the counties to the north of the Midlands, such re-deployments could be effective and frequently, they certainly brought a better result than could have resulted from any other form of deployment strategy. The staff officers were able to identify and warn relevant forces of impending problem areas, and to afford ready access to adequate resources with which to confront those problems. This was especially important as further forces began to suffer the problem of large-scale and violent picketing activity. All operational command, of course, remained with the force in which activity was taking place, but the ready availability of the required mutual aid, often anticipated from within the NRC, proved an invaluable asset to police commanders on the ground.

The greater level of activity requiring the re-deployment of mutual aid PSUs was certainly encountered during the early morning 'wind-down' period but the staff on the controller side of the NRC monitored demands throughout the twenty-four hours. The staff officers maintained an overview to determine whether any mutual aid units could and should be re-deployed, and if so, which. This practice, with the staff officers being the consistent factors, removed any loss of continuity that would, otherwise, have been possible through the weekly changes of staff on the controller side of the NRC. It also, of course, placed a considerable focus upon the roles of the staff officers who consequently became committed to the task over the full duration of this activation of the Centre.

In the latter months of 1984 the ACPO General Purposes Committee, recognising the demands that the long activation had placed, and still was having, on the two staff officers, invited chief constables of forces around London to nominate potentially suitable superintendents to attend the NRC for a week each to be introduced to the staff officer role. Four such superintendents attended on successive weeks. Their assistance to the incumbent staff officers was not outweighed by the additional commitment that imparting some of the information gained over the previous more than six months placed upon the two. It was also evident that week-by-week involvement was no substitute for the continuity of involvement that the two incumbent staff officers were able to offer.

Most chief constables with troublesome colliery gates to supervise, appointed superintendents to take the role of police commander for an area. Sometimes this was for one colliery where there was a severe threat of violent intimidation, and in other instances these superintendents would assume an area command, covering a number of collieries. Within the first month of the pressures on these policing contingents, it became evident that the relatively low numbers of officers in this rank available within many of the affected forces was resulting in an extreme and stress-inducing pressure on these officers. Consequently, the request was made to the NRC for weekly deployments of officers of superintendent rank on aid to these forces.

The requirement was, initially, filled by those superintendents that the chief officers of the supplying force thought they could most readily afford to lose for a week at a time: often those involved in administrative and training duties. Not all these officers had completed the only recently introduced Regional Command Band Public Order Courses, and negotiation with ACPO officers in the supplying forces changed this to ensure that the most suitably equipped and experienced superintendents filled the roles. The relative shortage of 'Command Band' trained officers was simply one of timescale. These courses had been devised by a mixed Metropolitan and provincial team working at the Metropolitan Police Hendon training school and in liaison with the Public Order Forward Planning Unit only months before the NUM Dispute had started. Some, but not all, regional training courses had started by the outset of the NUM move to strike action, but there were only a relatively small number of superintendents who had benefited from the courses. In the few years immediately after 1985, virtually all officers in the ranks of chief inspector, superintendent, and chief superintendent participated in this regional training.

Quite early in the Dispute and recognising his inability to simultaneously remain in command of his own force and adequately offer direct management support to the NRC staff officers, the president enlisted the assistance of his ACPO colleagues from around the Home Counties. The deputy chief constable of Cambridgeshire took on the coordinating role for the supply to the NRC of a deputy chief constable on each weekday morning, replacing the ACPO president who had previously attempted to fulfil this role as often as possible. Although there was good support from forces as distant as Northamptonshire, some nearer to London did not participate. The deputy of Cambridgeshire devised a rota and, to his great credit and with the cooperation of his chief constable, he filled those days when no other deputy chief was available. The rapidly acquired expertise of the staff officers made the hands-on involvement of these deputy chief constables minimal, but they proved to be an asset in two main areas. They offered an ACPO presence during the parts of the day most likely to see visits to the NRC by Home Office ministers, visiting chief officers, from the UK and abroad, and for the mass media. They also gave an authoritative ACPO voice when required in the negotiation with forces, and usually when the large numbers of mutual aid commitments were being addressed for the following week.

The five or six officers who on a regular basis filled this role found their days at the NRC useful on a personal level. It gave them some distance from the immediate demands of their own offices, and afforded time to reflect upon some of their paperwork without too much hindrance. Their relationship with the staff officers was one not easily encountered within their own forces and was of benefit on both sides.

From the first week, the media interest in the NUM Dispute, and especially the policing reaction, was considerable. It was realised very early that the presentation of the policing of the Dispute on television news bulletins was an important aspect with regards to a public relations standpoint. A television console, with recording capability, was introduced to the NRC for the first time and news bulletins recorded so that they could be examined if thought appropriate. Similarly, copies of all national newspapers were brought into the NRC and reviewed by the information officer each morning. On several occasions television reporters and camera crews were allowed access. Care was taken to ensure that the wall displays that appeared 'on camera' were only those which the staff in the Centre wanted revealed. In particular, the displays of available mutual aid units were never allowed to be broadcast. It must be said that the approach taken by the president of ACPO, from the early days and through into the next presidential incumbency, was one of being as open to the media as was operationally sensible.

At all levels in the UK, and from all over the world, the press, radio, and television contact with the NRC was largely handled by the staff officers and Metropolitan Police inspector, information officer. The early morning and periodic contact with media researchers proved to be of mutual benefit; but there were perhaps inevitably some occasions when this 'open-door' approach was abused. A recurring theme from the media was that of the NRC being the forerunner of a national police force for the UK. History has of course proved the lie, but at the time the rebuttal from ACPO was that the existence of the NRC demonstrably made a national force unnecessary. The ability of forces to co-operate, share resources, and have them coordinated through the NRC, removed any potential perceived benefit of the UK moving to a national police force. The politically driven efforts to move away from local police forces that appeared again in the early twenty-first century identified that there remains a strong feeling in the service and in the wider community for policing to be locally centred. The benefits of the national police force in Scotland remains an open question. In the main, the accessibility for media reporters and researchers was appreciated by them, and of some importance in getting across the true role of the NRC, but there were exceptions.

Later in the Dispute, in the Autumn of 1984 as more colliery areas were seeing miners identifying their wish to return to work, one national daily newspaper contacted the NRC on an afternoon and enquired of one of the staff officers, requesting a quote on the changing scenario. The current situation as seen from the NRC, was – as had become customary – given openly and honestly. When the information officer reviewed the papers the following morning, the quote from the staff officer was centre front page. The first two paragraphs after the opening quote marks were an accurate reflection of what had been said but, without closing inverted commas, another two paragraphs read as though the officer had stated an operational control involvement by the NRC. That morning the deputy chief constable had arrived from his Cambridgeshire base early and, after discussing the matter with the staff officer, spoke with the editor of the newspaper involved. The consequence was that the editor was told that there would be no further information imparted to any representatives of his newspaper. This was adhered to, but open contact was still maintained with other newspapers, none of which chose to breach the trust built up. It is highly likely that the breach which had occurred must have been the subject of some regret by the editor concerned.

Conversely, a national Sunday newspaper had a team of reporters and researchers who produced longer articles for their magazine section, and sought interviews with the NRC officers. The view taken by the staff officers and, largely, supported by ACPO was that the service was doing a good job under, probably unprecedented, difficult circumstances and had nothing to hide from the wider public. The product of these interviews was a not entirely supportive, but well balanced, magazine article on the policing of the dispute as one of a series on the Dispute itself. This team, later, produced their findings in book form.[4]

The early introduction of the television equipment and access to daily newspapers was a useful external support to the massive flow of information being exchanged with the affected forces across the country. Following his early arrival each weekday morning, the Metropolitan Police inspector who assumed the role of information officer throughout the activation, set about gathering the reports from around the affected areas. In succession, two young ladies, and one other very briefly, were provided from the secretarial staff within NSY and they, along with the information officer, became accustomed to working a long day. Word processing equipment was quite a new innovation in 1984, and the machine used in support of the NRC's activity was brought down from

---

[4] Sunday Times Insight Team (1985) *Strike: Thatcher, Scargill and the Miners* London: Harper Collins

Cambridgeshire. Each morning one of the staff officers dictated the president's *daily incident report* to be typed directly into the word processor from notes provided, often directly as the details came in, by the information officer. Arrangements were made, after the first week, for copies of the printed pages to be replicated within NSY and supplied to a relatively few additional people.

Each morning at about 0900 hours, as the report came off the press, the Home Office representative arrived at the NRC and was briefed by the staff officers and handed a copy of the *president's report*. Just as the media interest soon developed, so more critically did that of politicians. At that time, Prime Minister's question time was traditionally on a Thursday, as parliament started its rather oddly timed working day. After only a few such sessions, where the Prime Minister was receiving questions on the progress of the NUM Dispute, the demands for information were of course focused upon the ready source emanating from the NRC.

Soon a pattern arose of the staff officers gathering weekly information on criminal and other activities across the country and presenting them in a 'Return of Statistical Information'. This task started midday on each Wednesday and the report was assembled on the word processor on behalf of the president of ACPO. Civil servants in the private office of the Home Secretary took delivery of the report each Wednesday evening and used the information it contained to assist in formulating the responses for the Prime Minister for the following day. It was not unusual for this process to run well into the evening and, with the early starts generated by the dynamic mutual aid redeployments, Wednesdays became an even longer day for the staff officers. The *Return of Statistical Information* is so revealing of what the NUM Dispute involved that it warrants an appendix (appendix 5) of its own. Some of the description of what these statistics meant in real terms is contained in chapter 5 and reflected in the figures presented in appendices 6 and 7.

The demands, both in terms of concentration of effort and elongation of sustaining that effort had never before been experienced, nor could they have been anticipated. There were regular returns by many of the Metropolitan officers working in the National Reporting Centre each week, some coming back every three or four weeks from their normal duties, but others spent only a short time in the NRC. To give some idea of the numbers, by the Christmas of 1984 over 100 individual Metropolitan officers had performed some amount of duty in the NRC. As mentioned earlier, the only constantly committed of the Metropolitan officers was the inspector who filled the role of information officer - from the first couple of weeks through to the end of the activation. He was closely followed in terms of time spent in the Centre by the second of the secretaries, who brought with her not only a charm and sense of humour but also the distinct advantage, when long hours were demanded, of living just around the proverbial corner in Westminster. Most of the relatively small number of deputy chief constables were seen in the NRC repeatedly, with the deputy from Cambridgeshire doing much more than his share of this duty. Inevitably, and of the considerable benefit to the policing operations across the country, this small group formed a most advantageous working relationship with their more junior ranked colleagues.

Until the scenario in South Wales started to change as 1985 dawned, the two staff officers worked long hours from Sunday evening through to Friday and really only enjoyed one day a week at home throughout the year. In the January of 1985, with violent picketing and other extremes of activity, the chief constable of the South Wales Police was compelled to request that the superintendent be returned to his force. In the school summer holidays each of the staff officers were relieved for a week, but to accomplish this, the other had to carry the tasks alone. Not until much later in the activation was the consideration given to training others for this role and this, as has already been said, was not entirely satisfactory. The essence of their roles was that they provided the continuity factor throughout the fifty-one weeks of the operation. When the superintendent returned to South Wales, the Chief Constable of the Avon and Somerset Constabulary, Ronald Broome, was prevailed upon by the president of ACPO – who from September 1984 was Chief Constable of Nottinghamshire Charles MacLachlan, to temporarily promote his inspector who was there. With the fast-changing situation, where so many more miners were returning to work, the demands within the NRC had reduced such that this staff officer, now with the rank of chief inspector, was enabled to continue the role alone.

The less regular requirements for mutual aid assistance, related to more specialist support and included mounted and dog handler officers. In 1984 there were still a number of forces where a small mounted section existed and the Metropolitan Police mounted branch then had 130 horses, stabled in a number of locations around London. Across the country, these officers and their steeds had largely been used for the policing of crowds attending football matches in their respective areas. Their more localised, but quite frequent deployment on mutual aid in support of neighbouring forces, meant that they were usually capable of transporting at least a significant proportion of their horses with their own horse boxes. Dog transport is a daily requirement, and all forces had the means to convey animals and their handlers as a matter of routine deployment. Since the street disorders in 1980/81, many, if not all mounted officers and dog handlers had received some training to augment their years of football policing experience for their deployment in these, even more violent, situations. The *Tactical Options Manual* produced by the POFPU had been distributed, in its initial form, to all chief officers in 1983 and contained 'best practice' advice on such deployments in the more politically sensitive disorder situations away from the football hooligan scenario.

A View from the Centre

The deployment of large numbers of officers as PSUs presented a varied approach in terms of logistics. Within a few weeks of the residential aid programme starting, it became customary for some forces to return to the same supported force on a regular basis. This enabled those with longer distances to travel to avoid the discomfort and relative expense of using the protected personnel carriers that were necessary for their operational deployments in the colliery areas. It became quite common for the carriers to remain in the 'host' force and for the officers forming that week's contingent to be transported over the longer journeys in more comfortable coaches. One force,

Accommodating the Demands

Hampshire, even used internal flights to take their personnel up to the northern forces they were supporting.

In summation, the NRC and the principles of mutual aid between police forces, as it was set up following the guidance from the problems from the 1970s, proved fit for the overall purpose. Many innovative measures were added to the earlier formula, most within the first few days and weeks. That the NRC proved to be the coordination answer to any thought that the police forces in England and Wales could not cope, is beyond doubt.

A View from the Centre

Spiked staves embedded into the ground to deter mounted officers. Like police PSU tactics, the demonstrators also learnt from history.

Accommodating the Demands

Makeshift barricades

5. The Operational Demands

Chapter three outlined the initial requirements that the move to strike action by the National Union of Mineworkers brought upon the police. The dispute itself was heavily politically motivated and strenuous efforts were made, by the NUM leadership, some politicians and others, to include the police in the politics of the situation. At that time, the police service in England and Wales (and Scotland, although outside this remit) was proud of a long tradition of remaining aloof from political interference. Few politicians, even now that we have elected Police & Crime Commissioners, see their role as to involve themselves directly in operational matters, it is, after all, much safer to offer post-incident comment. The only exception that the author can identify of a Home Secretary being on the streets during a 'live' incident was early in 1911 at the 'Siege of Sidney Street' in London's West End. The Home Secretary at the time was one Winston Churchill, who issued direct instructions to responding police, fire and army personnel.

In 1984 – 85, the police leadership, in the guise of the Association of Chief Police Officers and its president, were determined to police the situation, however extreme and politicised it became, in the even handed manner of the traditional British model – without fear or favour. Whatever was said at the time and has been said since, an objective assessment will show that this endeavour was, in large measure, achieved.

The Operational Demands

Within this chapter and appendices 5A - D, the reader may gain some idea as to what it was that had to be confronted over that most demanding of years.

The figures are, themselves, not the only measure of what became the full extent and variety of the demands placed upon the police officers, both in their own force areas and when on mutual aid. There is also a need for a cautionary warning that the figures were believed to be significantly reduced by the reluctance of many members of communities to report criminal activity perpetrated against them. This was partly through a sense of loyalty, even though in disagreement with the principle of the strike many still did not want to resort to the law when a victim. It was also due to straight victimisation, with those subjected to violent or threatening behaviour remaining too intimidated to seek assistance from the police. The violence and intimidation was between neighbours and within communities, where both loyalties, and pressures, ran deep.

The violence of some more public confrontations between working and striking miners, with the police seeking to 'hold the ring', received significant publicity through all forms of the media. Even more likely to receive significant media attention were any incidents where strenuous police activity had become necessary – often after long, unreported, periods during which much effort was applied by demonstrators in the effort to goad police officers. Unfortunately, much less attention was given, at the time and since, to the even more insidious intimidation that many ordinary people encountered within split mining communities.

A View from the Centre

The hidden aspect of the NUM Dispute of 1984 – 85, one which has never been adequately reflected in any of the analyses attempted but which received substantial policing attention in a (largely impossible) attempt to quell it, was this intimidatory activity within the wider communities. Taking the children to school was a trial of character for many working miners' wives. The children's experiences in their playgrounds and on the streets around their homes, when their parents permitted them to go out to play, must have scarred some emotionally for the remainder of their lives. The general feeling of total isolation suffered by the families of the few working miners in many areas must have made principle seem a very costly virtue. These aspects cannot be measured by any statistic, but they were, without doubt, the real cost for many of the unilateral NUM declaration that a strike was appropriate. Even now, to avoid continuing to be further 'singled out', few of those who were victims of intimidation are prepared to declare just how much they and their families were damaged.

The romanticised image of the miner has, not just in 1984 – 85, been exaggerated beyond measure; but that hard work, in a team, in the stifling heat of the depths of the earth, does require strength of character must be beyond doubt. Those (in some areas very few) who revealed that particular inner strength by refusing to be forced to accept a decision taken from the corridors of the NUM offices without their entitlement to being consulted, paid a high price – then and afterwards. Their refusal to be the pawns of an NUM leadership that had made no secret of the political intentions of the dispute was not destined to bring them credit when the majority were so indoctrinated into accepting the union view. Even, decades further on, little has been said of the sheer bravery of many of these men and their immediate families for their desire to resist a dictatorial pressure which, to their eternal shame, was supported by the intimidatory, threatening and, even, violent behaviour of those who saw only the old fashioned struggle.

Within the context of the multi-faceted and many confrontations that needed to receive police attention, there was a political thread which perceived seeking to discredit that policing activity, as an entirely legitimate tactic. That there were unquestionably excesses on the part of individual police officers on occasions deserves no excuse but may, perhaps, be understood when there were so many, often sustained, efforts to provoke such overreaction. The levels of violence delivered by some groups, often not all striking miners but including a wide range of others who saw the opportunity to 'have a go', were, too often, of an order only previously witnessed in recent times in the riotous behaviour in the inner-city areas of 1980 and 1981.

For many striking miners the expenses they received for being prepared to leave their homes very early in the morning and be transported wherever their leaders decided was the target for the flying pickets for that day, was their only income beyond whatever state benefits their family responsibilities brought their way. Consequently, many were quite restrained in their actions as the often small numbers of working miners were escorted past them at the colliery gate. Indeed the atmosphere at many picket lines was quite jovial and striking miners often shared the warmth from their improvised braziers with the police officers stationed there to hold them back, while the working miners entered. This understanding of each other's roles, almost bonhomie, between police officers and striking miners was, of course, not often visible when the media were present. It was not unusual for there to be much pushing and shoving while the cameras were in evidence and for it to cease as soon as the reporting teams had moved on to their next assignment.

The most extreme violence was seen when there was some evident orchestration from local or national leaders, and when the striking miners were bolstered by others, often more politically motivated and sometimes less constrained than the local miner with a family to consider.

Where striking miners did go far beyond any concept of peaceful picketing it is, perhaps, capable of being understood through the extremes of frustration they must have felt as the weeks turned into months. Many had wives and young families to consider, and the pride which they traditionally took in providing a reasonable standard of living through their hard labour, must have been severely dented. The breadth of those from without the mining industry who also saw fit to involve themselves in unlawful activity during this fifty-one-week period can be gauged from the appendix 5B. Of course, when on the pickets, there was nothing to distinguish striking miners, to those with no direct stake in the Dispute.

Throughout the months of the overtime ban, and the increasingly apparent likelihood of strike action being the next move by the NUM, the Energy Ministry had been careful to ensure that stocks of fuel at coal-powered electricity generating stations were backed-up to considerable capacity. It was therefore with some confidence that the Ministry perceived that it could sustain electricity supplies even though the coal production had dwindled. This was, of course, in the expectation of a relatively short strike, but that was not to become the scenario.

After several weeks of the national mining production having been severely curtailed, the move to import coal became an inevitable alternative option. Although not the only such port, Immingham, on the estuary of the river Humber, became a focus of attention – partly because of the need for the coal to be transported by road to the coking plant near Sheffield. The policing of the convoys of lorries attracted much attention from the NUM and both sites were heavily picketed on many occasions. This was a somewhat different policing requirement in that a degree of security had to be offered to the lorries while in transit, as well as at each end of their journey. A similar situation occurred in South Wales, between the docks at Port Talbot and the steelworks at Llanwern, for which support had to be made available from nearby forces. Although it was only once called upon for deployment, the pressures upon the South Wales Constabulary from not accepting more widely resourced assistance were, as described earlier, considerable.

The NUM leadership remembered well, as did the police service, the success they had found in mounting a blockade of the Saltley Depot in Birmingham a decade earlier. It became apparent that they were seeking to achieve the same political impact upon the democratically elected government at the Orgreave coking plant near Sheffield in June of 1984.

With a strong presence of the illegal[5] flying pickets anticipated at Orgreave on the following Monday, the numbers of mutual aid units and mounted officers planned for allocation to the South Yorkshire Police were increased. When the staff officers returned to New Scotland Yard on the evening of Sunday 17th June, there were still requests for further units coming in from the South Yorkshire force, and those further enhancements required some considerable effort in the NRC and much activity in the forces asked to supply the manpower.

The fears of the chief constable in South Yorkshire had not been misplaced, and by far the most strenuous single day of violent activity was around the Orgreave coking plant on 18th June 1984. The efforts of the previous week, and activity facilitated by the NRC and supplying forces over the weekend, had produced what was the largest single day's deployment of mutual aid. By far the largest contingent were allocated to South Yorkshire, but the numbers that had become relatively settled upon in the other forces around that area were, in most cases, maintained. South Yorkshire received 164 PSUs (3,772 officers) late on the Sunday or overnight and with a further total of 186 PSUs (4,278 Officers) on deployment to other forces. With four units (92 officers) in Kent, this brought the full number of PSU contingents to a nationwide total of 8,142 officers on the morning

---

[5] S.17 Employment Act 1980

of Monday 18th June 1984. Much of this mobilisation consisted of fully public order-equipped PSUs, but there was also a significant deployment of mounted officers to the South Yorkshire force, requested because of the open country around the coke works.

Blessed with a resolute Chief Constable, Peter Wright, South Yorkshire also had a strong and able Assistant Chief Constable (Operations) Tony Clement, who was supported by a group of experienced senior officers. South Yorkshire was the NUM leadership's home territory, and these officers were well versed in what that leadership could achieve in terms of mobilising large numbers who would do their bidding. While there had been many occasions in the three months of the partial strike in which a recognised police tactic had been to seek to restrict the movements of the flying pickets before reaching their unlawful assemblies, no such effort was made in the early morning of 18th June on the approach to the Orgreave plant. The constant efforts on the part of the police in this and other colliery areas had been to seek to follow through their sworn duty to prevent breaches of the Queen's Peace.

On this occasion, and made possible by the efforts that had been input at the NRC and within many forces asked to supply support, the police manpower was available for a confrontation that the police hoped would mark an end to a three-month catalogue of violence and intimidation. That it did not, despite the immediate policing objective of securing access to the plant being achieved, speaks volumes for the ability of the NUM leadership to motivate large numbers of their membership to support their aims. The lasting impact, of course, was a singular demonstration that the police service, through coordination of effort and sound command leadership, could meet even this strong a challenge to the rule of law in the country.

It cannot be identified that the Violence at Orgreave marked a turning point in the Dispute, largely because the media images were used, by those who wanted to see it continue, as evidence that the mining community was, somehow, under threat from the government. This tactic worked well enough with such a strong history of unionism and total disregard for the economics within the available debate. What it did do was to make it evident that the violence resorted to by such groups, no matter how large, could be successfully confronted and would not succeed. It certainly made the movement of iron ore and coal/coke between Port Talbot and Llanwern in South Wales seem feasible, and those convoys commenced that same week.

In the aftermath, the levels of violence and intimidation in mining communities became even more of a focus. It was, after all, less visible – to the police at least – for working miners to be placed under threat through actions against their wives and children, than it was to confront them at the colliery gate. These intimidatory tactics by striking members of the NUM were to work against the Union's rhetoric, when combined with the visible evidence that miners returning to work were receiving the required levels of protection to enter at the colliery gates. As the second quarter of the Dispute dragged on, so more, sometimes isolated, individual miners saw the futility of blind obedience to the union leaders and followed the example of their Nottinghamshire and the few more local free-minded and not a little courageous, colleagues.

The very gradual and disjointed return of small numbers of miners to their collieries continued through the summer and into the autumn, but the strength of the NUM adherence by the majority was such that the process was exceedingly slow. Although there were strenuous confrontations early in the Dispute (on 12th & 19th April 1984) outside St James House in South Yorkshire, it was not until late August that a small number of miners sought to return to work in the Yorkshire area. In Derbyshire there were two distinct coal mining areas. The southern part adhered to the Nottinghamshire example while those miners in the northern part fell in line with their Yorkshire colleagues. The North Wales coalfield miners stopped work initially but soon held their own local ballot and within a few weeks about 90% of the miners had returned to work. Their very isolation from the other areas meant that they received relatively little attention. Conversely, in South Wales the support for the NUM was, for many months and at least overtly, completely solid and, again, no real violence was encountered until late in the year.

There was an unrelated, although impactive, situation in Sussex in early September. With the Conservative Party conference scheduled in Brighton, the NRC allocated PSUs in support of the local force. They were to encounter a challenge not wholly expected, when the IRA detonated a bomb in the hotel being used by the leaders of the party. The Prime Minister, evidently the intended target, was uninjured. Some media speculation in the immediate aftermath surrounding concerns that the explosion was some extreme escalation of the NUM Dispute, were soon dismissed. At this distance in time and with the changes so welcomed in Northern Ireland, it is easy to forget that mainland Britain had been subjected to such intermittent terrorist activity for much of the fifteen years preceding the Brighton bombing. In the Conference Hall the following morning, the Prime Minister demonstrated that even such a personalised attack would no more succeed than had similar earlier atrocities.

In the autumn, for the first time in the more than six months of the Dispute, miners in the South Wales coalfield started to return to work, at first in very small numbers. The convoys between Humberside and South Yorkshire and those across South Wales had been, obviously, vulnerable to attack from over-bridges along their routes. Although police attention had been afforded in an attempt to prevent this method of attack upon these convoys, it was an impossible task to secure every route being taken by miners going to work. On 30th November 1984, three striking miners attacked a taxi taking one of the early returning miners to work. The miner escaped injury but the taxi driver was killed. The impact of this action on the fair-minded miners in South Wales and elsewhere was not without significance. That this was the only example of a death at another's hand during this fifty-one-week Dispute is, perhaps, more to do with good fortune than any regard for the importance of human life in some quarters. Albeit, countless numbers of lives were ruined or permanently scarred in myriad other ways too.

The activities of striking miners, and their wide variety of cohorts from outside the coal industry, is well reflected in a publication distributed in October 1984 by the National Working Miners Committee. This publication catalogues some of the extent of the threat under which working miners and their families lived through large parts of this fifty-one-week Dispute. The information in this publication is referred to in the following chapter and detailed in appendix 7. It is a source of real sadness that some, of the antagonistic feelings and activities within the mining communities survived long after 1985, some remaining problematic for a full return to a cohesive community even to the present day. Such deep-held enmity is, for example, believed to have been a significant contributory factor in a murder by a working miner named Robert Boyer, of his neighbour Keith Frogson, a former stalwart Union man, in a Nottinghamshire mining town as late as 2004.

To sum up the operational demands of policing the 1984 – 85 National Union of Mineworkers Dispute, it has to be reasonable to state that the police service has never been so severely tested, and proved itself to be so capable. Mass confrontations were met with sufficient numbers of police officers to ensure no lasting impact on the rule of law as opposed to mob rule, and a policing presence was maintained in stressed communities, such that only the most insidious intimidatory activities could have any wider than isolated effect. That the working, or intending to work, miners and their families were so severely pressurised was more a mark of shame on the perpetrators than a failing of the policing effort.

The Operational Demands

A View from the Centre

6. Social and Economic Implications

Just as appears to be the case in respect of many international struggles in which the country has been involved over the years, so too the overall cost of the NUM Dispute in 1984 – 85 does not seem to have been totalled, although estimates put it somewhere in the region of £200m. That it was a considerable sum is without doubt. There is, of course, the possibility that this short-term expenditure was not significant in terms of what it would have cost to have kept all the collieries that were operating in 1983 producing ever more expensive coal until more recent times.

The operational demands of the unlawful, and in too many cases violent, picketing activity were encountered, by virtue of the location of the collieries where miners wanted to continue or return to work, in only about a dozen of the forty-three police forces that had been in existence since the politically driven local authority boundary changes of April 1974. The most severe impact was only experienced in about half of those dozen forces, with Nottinghamshire Constabulary the worst affected. The financial arrangements relating to the supply of mutual aid had followed on from the capability for such provision in the *Police Act 1964*. In essence, this required that basic hours of duty were not accounted but overtime and other ancillary costs, such as travel and subsistence, were re-claimable from the force receiving the aid.

A View from the Centre

From the first few weeks, it was evident that the costs falling to those forces encountering the greatest need to call upon support were reaching sums that their police authorities could not possibly meet. Government ministers were not alone in their amazement, stated or not, at the capacity of the police service to adequately confront this, scarcely disguised, lurch towards potential anarchy. They soon declared that central government funding support would be made available, above the customary local expectation of an additional penny on the Rates.

This type of central government support was not unusual and had traditionally been applied to a wide range of abnormal policing commitments over the years. By the time that this matter was being addressed within government, it had already been the case that such numbers of police officers were being supplied by forces without collieries that an unusual additional provision was made in this instance. The capacity for forces supplying mutual aid to claim for 'consequential' costs was written in to the provisions. Only those forces confronting the problem in their own territory directly claimed the additional central funding but those forces supplying the assistance, in whatever form, charged it to the force they were supporting.

It emerged however some twenty years later, with letters between the Home Secretary, Sir Leon Brittan and Prime Minister Margaret Thatcher released in 2006, showing that the government had, at least to some degree, attempted to renege on this arrangement. Letters from Brittan's aides to Thatcher's suggested that "it would be wrong in principle for central government to pay the full costs: policing is essentially a local matter". "One of the advantages of leaving forces to pay ... gives them an incentive to economise." It seems that only after significant pressure from elected officials in Nottinghamshire especially, where a majority of miners continued working and were thus able to effectively undermine the strike action sufficiently, that the government eventually relented. It was not until the Conservative Party conference in October 1984 that Sir Leon finally committed to the central government funding.[6]

Not all forces supplying assistance availed themselves fully of the 'consequential costs' provision, although some did in full measure. It has to be said that, for the benefit of their home public and rate payers, all should have taken up this offer in full. It allowed for those forces supplying mutual aid to in-fill within their own communities by resort to officers working extended hours to maintain the policing cover unavoidably reduced by their colleagues being sent to the colliery areas.

By this provision there were a number of major benefits not available under the normal mutual aid charging arrangements. The communities in the colliery areas were afforded as much protection as could be achieved and those in the rest of the country were not disadvantaged. For those chief police officers who made full use of the provision, their ability to 'keep faith' with their local communities was undiminished, indeed in some areas the extended working actually provided enhanced local policing cover. For the patrol level officers there was an opportunity for overtime payments, albeit on a lesser

---

[6] *The Guardian* 3rd January 2006

scale, even if they were not deployed on mutual aid. This latter aspect became important for morale in forces, where only the fully public order trained officers were being sent on the mutual aid commitments. It served to mitigate the wide disparity of net income between those travelling to the colliery areas and those, often hard-pressed, who tried to maintain policing cover in their home forces.

Over the fifty-one weeks of the NUM Dispute, there were few police officers in the ranks between constable and chief inspector who did not benefit financially, and some to a considerable degree. Officers in these ranks are known within the service as the federated ranks because it is at these levels within the service where there is eligibility to be a member of the Police Federation. At that time it was rare for officers not to be members of the Police Federation. Officers in the superintending and chief officer ranks were not eligible for overtime payments, the salary scales reflecting this under normal circumstances, and superintendents working extended hours both as colliery commanders and elsewhere were often receiving a lower 'net' monthly pay than many, if not most, of their subordinate officers. There was an examination of this anomaly and consideration was given to some form of temporary allowance but there was no mechanism for it to be implemented under the *Police Pay Regulations*.

There was the further consideration within the *Police Regulations* which had gradually been amended over many years, to improve the impact of police work on domestic circumstances and which had a cost implication within the residential aid

Social and Economic Implications

situation. The situation whereby police officers had originally held no entitlement to rest days had long passed, and those officers of federated ranks had reached the agreement under the *Regulations* whereby their rest days were protected for predictability within seven days of their scheduled rostering. Where officers were required to work on such a day but had not received eight days' notice, they were entitled not only to overtime payment for the whole day but also to have another rest day allocated as further compensation. With the demands of the commitment to supplying such large numbers of officers on mutual aid, this condition was often difficult to satisfy without such compensatory conditions coming into play.

Although the financial situation for so many police officers looked good throughout the NUM Dispute, there were other aspects of their deployments which were not so positive. Police officers were generally popular and appreciated, at least in the abstract sense, with the wider population recognising the important role police officers play within society. They are also, of course, accustomed to being less popular with some of those members of society with whom they come into contact on an individual basis. This situation was exaggerated for those officers on mutual aid, for they were identified as not being part of the local community. This phenomenon was recognisable even within local forces, where support group officers were called upon to assist local patrol officers. In the politically and socially charged circumstances of the policing requirements of many colliery areas it was heavily accentuated. The fact that many of the mutual aid officers were housed for a week at a time in barracks type accommodation served only to further highlight this unusual situation of isolation from the community.

On the domestic front there were inevitable difficulties too. Police officers' families traditionally become accustomed to the unsocial hours lifestyle associated with working rotating shift patterns, including nights, and to the unpredictability of their time at home. But they are used to seeing dad about at some time on most days. During the NUM Dispute, the contact with their families was necessarily and significantly reduced. Some forces dealt with this in as understanding a manner as they could achieve, some sending welfare officers with their mutual aid contingents, and also providing welfare support for the families back at home. Other forces, perhaps too many, did nothing. The additional income, especially if employed wisely, was some compensation for this massive disruption to the lives of many police officers' families – but not always enough to prevent permanent damage to relationships.

For the mineworkers and their families times could be, and often were even more difficult, and in many cases devastating. The much vaunted and quite widely overplayed mining community spirit was of support to some, but like a viper in the bosom to others. In the few areas where the whole local community had determined not to follow the diktat of the NUM, there was local support to stand up against the marauding miners (and, as always, others) that descended upon them with irregular monotony. In the mining communities where the illegal strike was being followed to a man, the community was very strong and supported by others from across the country who saw their plight, even if they did not see the political dangers which had induced it.

The real problems were for those who chose to show the independence of character for which the miner had been held up as an example over many years. These, sometimes single in number as well as in mind, were the ones who suffered most throughout this Dispute, despite the fact that they were the only ones bringing home a wage. The self-respect that these families felt for having not been dictated to and being able to pay their own way was poor recompense for having to withstand the taunts, threats, and even violence from their neighbours; sometimes even from members of their own families. The only tangible support for the miners who chose to continue, or return to, working and, perhaps more importantly, their families, were the police officers who were resident in or deployed to their areas. But no police presence could remove the immense social pressures that these families were forced to endure, often by people who once they thought were colleagues and friends.

The strength of the NUM had been perceived by its members over the years as its support for workers in an industry which could have devastating effects upon individuals. The days of the struggle against the mean colliery owners had long-since disappeared and the nationalisation of the bulk of the coal mining industry had brought massive and prolonged subsidy to keep these men in work, even where the economics of the situation pointed to such investment as being downright wasteful. The miner had a general respect from those majority of citizens who knew that they could not, would not, do such a dirty and dangerous job. Indeed, it is unlikely that there would have been so little public outcry at the amount of public money this industry consumed had this respect not been so widely held. The expectation of the miner in normal circumstances was that the NUM was there for support in times of difficulty or tragedy. It was also an expectation within most trades' unions that if there was a vote to take strike action their consequent loss of earnings would be, at least partly, compensated from the coffers of the union through strike pay.

During the Dispute of 1984 – 85 the funds of the NUM were not used in this way. Instead, they were used against those members of the union who had chosen to continue working by being directed towards encouraging striking miners to travel within and beyond their own colliery areas in an effort to force their fellow union members to toe the line. These were not efforts to reinforce the backdrop of collective bargaining by peaceful picketing. The leadership of the NUM were not well known for a stance of peaceful negotiation, and the lack of a substance to the economics of keeping collieries open brought a perception, probably correctly, that only Violence would serve the more political intentions they espoused. However objectively it is attempted, it is difficult, even impossible, to fail to conclude that the intentions of the NUM leadership and their political supporters, were directed against the government of the day at least as much as any support for retaining miners' jobs. There was also little to indicate that the leadership of the NUM shared either the financial burden of the striking miners, or the peer pressure and violent intimidation of the working miner throughout this awful year.

Social and Economic Implications

Let there be no misunderstanding. This was a period which, in modern times in these islands, has not been equalled for its proximity to political anarchy. The attempt at the overthrow of yet another democratically elected government brought, of itself, a time at which the social structure of the nation was under severe threat. Worse, for those directly involved, the insidious effects of local peer pressures could be seen in their most naked and devastating embodiment. Only one factor stood between the worst potential outcome and the triumph of democratic rule, and the nation should be forever in gratitude to the thousands of police officers who held the line, under often extreme circumstances. That they were able to achieve what not even the government of the day thought was within their capabilities, is a testament to their devotion to the task, the right-minded determination of their chief officers and, not infrequently, personal courage both at the level of meeting Violence and in the face of media and political challenges.

The author can think of no better way of painting this picture for the historical record than by referring to the document produced by The National Working Miners Committee. Although a sheaf of reports reached the NRC on a daily basis throughout the 1984 – 85 activation of that Centre, it seems more appropriate, at such a distance in time, to reflect upon what fair-minded miners saw and reported as those months dragged on. Not surprisingly, there are no personalised credits to the booklet, dated 5th October 1984, and entitled *The Miners' Dispute - A Catalogue of Violence* published by The National Working Miners Committee, Market Place, Ripley,

Derbyshire. For the individuals who collated the information in the booklet to have included their names would have been foolhardy in the extreme. Although the writers are not identified, many of the pages of the document contain personal details, even home addresses, of those mentioned in some of its reported incidents. This is applied to both injured parties and perpetrators of violence and intimidation. These references to personal information have been eliminated in the appendix in which they appear here (7), but where they occurred the replacement term used has been placed in square brackets.

Although the compilers of this valuable document are unknown to this author, he wishes to record not only his sincere acknowledgement for the information but his profound respect for their courage under severe pressures at that time. The National Working Miners Committee encompassed miners from many collieries throughout the country and hence included those in Scotland for which the NRC had no remit.

The journal is divided into three sections, entitled - 'Attacks on Working Miners and Working Miners' Property', 'Attacks on the Police and Police Property' and 'Attacks on National Coal Board Staff and Property'. As the intention in appendix 7 is to provide the chronology of what was occurring, these incidents are recorded by date and from each section of the journal.

The frontispiece to the paper reads:

"From the first day of this dispute until 7am Wednesday 3rd October [1984], 7121 persons have been arrested for offences in connection with the dispute, 790 police officers have been injured, of who 65 suffered serious injuries, 2 miners have committed suicide, 2 have died as a result of picket line violence and 255 miners have been reported injured."

The introduction is reproduced in full, as it provides a valuable picture of the perception that was held by the NWMC:

> "The working miners are in the front line of the fight for freedom and democracy in Britain today.
>
> Since the beginning of this dispute every working miner, every day, as he leaves his home to go to work, must face the possibility that his wife, his children, his family will be abused, threatened, or even attacked whilst he is away.
>
> The National Working Miners Committee was formed to assist working miners and wanting-to-work miners to assert their right to work and to provide compensation for loss or injury.
>
> We have published this catalogue of Violence to remind political leaders, union leaders and members of the public that the operations of the present leadership of our union, the systematic intimidation,

the planned attacks, the unplanned violence arising out of the miners' dispute has led to unprecedented hardship, injury and material loss for significant numbers of ordinary working people - miners, their families, police officers, their families - as well as very considerable loss of and damage to property belonging to the National Coal Board, our employer.

The present leadership of the National Union of Mineworkers consistently blames the police for the violence. As will be seen from the evidence set out in this pamphlet, working miners and their property, National Coal Board employees and property have come under constant attack from striking miners since the beginning of the dispute.

This catalogue is not exhaustive. It could not be. Quite apart from the numerous unreported attacks and minor assaults on working miners we do not have the resources to compile an exhaustive catalogue. We would like to hear from any persons who are aware of incidents that are not set out in this pamphlet. We intend to publish further catalogues containing more information in the future.

This catalogue does not contain and could not contain a list of the thousands of threatening telephone calls, often late at night, often many times a night received by working miners or the hundreds

Social and Economic Implications

of thousands of personal threats of physical abuse endured by working miners and their families."

National Working Miners Committee, 5th October 1984

7. Legal Consequences

No comprehensive record exists for the outcome of the cases taken to court, as the process of legal actions continued beyond the end of the NRC activation; but the demand for information for the government during the activation brought a compilation of the figures for arrests and charges until 5th March 1985. As has already been said, these were presented, on behalf of the president of ACPO, to the private office of the Home Secretary each Wednesday evening. They were then reflected in a full brief to the Prime Minister, for use in responses at Question Time on the Thursday opening session in the House of Commons. The *Return of Statistical Information* was a cumulative document and identified the various aspects which had, from the first few weeks of Prime Minister's Question Time, become of Parliamentary, as well as national, interest.

Each week, the *Return* contained the numbers, as reported by forces to the NRC, of the categorisation, by nature of employment, of those arrested; the charges proffered against them; the results of cases currently completed and the picture regarding complaints received against police officers. In addition to the national statistics, each week the *Return* included a schedule for each affected force, with a breakdown of the figures as they applied in that area. Being cumulative, the *Return* grew steadily in size until it was more than 100 pages in length by its final edition. The various aspects of the offenders arrested, the nature of the charges proffered and the court results revealed before the closure of the NRC are reflected in appendices 5A - D. A synopsis of the returns relating to complaints against police officers is produced at appendices 6A & B.

The information reflected within this document is supported by personal reminders kept by the author throughout the NRC activation and for a short time later. The reports submitted from the NRC referred to within this document were, at the time of their production made available on a limited distribution. Those aspects used in PM's presentations were, of course, public and recorded as such. Following the closure of the NUM Dispute, the sizeable debrief, and the September 1985 ACPO conference, these papers were lodged at the Police College Library, Bramshill House, Hampshire and became available to all with access to that establishment. As these details constitute information presented to parliament and retained at Bramshill, they are already a part of public record, and therefore there is no harm in reproducing them summarily here.

In recent times the fear of crime has become a more recognised phenomenon, which can transcend the actual statistical possibility of being a victim. Although not frequently seen as a problem by 1984, it most certainly applied within many colliery communities. Those wishing to return to work sought mutual support across colliery areas by the formation of The National Working Miners Committee, based at Ripley in Derbyshire. They attempted to inform the wider public of this situation, which was so important to them, by the production in

A View from the Centre

October of 1984 of *The Miners' Dispute. A Catalogue of Violence*, aspects of which are reflected in appendix 7.

Should the opinion be believed that the National Union of Mineworkers Dispute of 1984 – 85 was no more than the miners' struggle to keep their jobs, barely more than a cursory scan through the contents of appendices 5 & 7 should dispel that perception. While an unpleasant experience for a large number of police officers, most of them were able to break away after each deployment to gain respite in their more supportive home surroundings - the exception was, of course, the police officers local to and living within the colliery areas. But those who suffered most were the working miners, or those expressing any desire to attend for work, and their families. Their suffering, even torment, was not only continuous throughout the period of the Dispute but would persist for long after the return to work in the week commencing 4th March 1985. The author feels that the appendices speak volumes on their own, with no need for any further comment.

8. Summary

Late in 1983, the Public Order Sub Committee of the ACPO General Purposes Committee was charged by that principal committee of the Association, with taking responsibility for the embryonic National Reporting Centre. The Public Order Forward Planning Unit, quite a unique working group created as an executive arm of the subcommittee, received the information and were charged with getting the NRC arrangements up to date and mounting an exercise for its operation. As has been said earlier, the previous activations of the National Reporting Centre had, since its inception a decade earlier, been few and of quite short duration.

The initial task of the POFPU had been the creation of the *Tactical Options Manual,* for the use by senior police officers in the event of large-scale public disorder, prompted by the street disturbances of 1980 and 1981. Although the initial issue of this large document had been accomplished in the summer of 1983, there were a considerable number of aspects which were still undergoing research. These were not only tactical manoeuvres but covered protective equipment for officers, animals, and vehicles. Since the POFPU was established in the autumn of 1982, the practice had been created for officers from provincial police forces to be selected by their chief constables to work alongside Metropolitan Police officers in the offices at New Scotland Yard. With a change of the superintendent in-post in early 1984, the provincial inspector was instructed to await the new man's arrival before working with him to establish a testing exercise for the NRC's operation.

With other matters to get to grips with the exercise papers for the NRC were only in the thought process stage when the NUM Dispute changed from its overtime ban of the previous six months, into an un-balloted call from the union leadership for strike action. Whatever the provincial superintendent and inspector on the POFPU may have invented as the mythical scenario for the intended exercise of the NRC, it would have been laughed at had it represented a tiny proportion of what was to become the reality for the NRC's next operational activation. Any meaningful exercise in anticipation of a large-scale policing operation must extend over a long enough timescale to include, as realistic as possible, a hand-over between shifts of staff but, in the main, this was accomplished by running exercises from one day into one other. The NUM Dispute activation was to run for 360 days!

This book has tried to paint the full picture of what was demanded of the police service in England and Wales over that, near, year of operation. In this last chapter, the author makes no apology for reiterating that the performance of the police service, the coordination of effort through ACPO, and the logistical and information flow support from the NRC, combined to produce a policing response beyond what anyone could have anticipated. In the early stages, there were obvious doubts from outside the police service, not least in parliamentary circles, as to whether the police would cope. In retrospect, even after the

Summary

passage of what is fast approaching a half of a century since the events, the organisation and individual bravery, moral as well as physical, of much of what policing involved over that year is difficult to wholly comprehend.

Following the extensive ACPO debrief of the policing arrangements for the NUM Dispute, the report from eleven working parties that informed that debrief was, unsurprisingly, the central theme of the ACPO conference in September 1985. Although the long series of operations throughout the Dispute and the support arrangements that backed them so well had been demonstrated to be entirely more than satisfactory, to have not deeply examined such an operation would have been at best foolhardy, and at worst a dereliction of what should be expected of the principal police officers. Several recommendations led to significant change. One example, assisted very much by the timing of the most current international radio frequency conference, was for all police vehicle radios to become fully capable of exchanging messages within all force areas.

The view taken was that the National Reporting Centre was somewhat of a confusing title for the facility at NSY and the new name arrived at was the Mutual Aid Coordination Centre (MACC). It must be said that this did not reflect the vital information exchanging role that the NRC had accomplished throughout the NUM Dispute, and that it had somewhat of a potential to be confused with the military acronym for Military Aid to the Civil Community. But, MACC it became.

A View from the Centre

The MACC was used, for monitoring only, in the late summer of 1985, when several large cities encountered a short-lived but serious resurgence of street disorders. It was, in 1987, used in the prisoner handling coordination role that had been seen in 1981. There have been other, short-term, activations since, but nothing on the scale of it's baptism of fire.

The conditions which applied both within the NRC and in the operational areas during the NUM Dispute in terms of hours worked may be problematic in any future activation of any length. The conditions of employment for police officers have been one of many changes within the service since the dawn of the new millennium. Although changes in *Police Regulations* have largely counterbalanced the potential benefits for serving police officers, the application of employment legislation has had significant impact upon what duties they can be required to perform. Just as throughout history police officers were, as Crown Officers, independent of any party political machine, so too were they, as not being employees, outside the employment legislation of the last quarter of the twentieth century.

That has all changed and, so too, may the capacity for an operation such as that undertaken in 1984 -85 to be repeated. It has to be hoped that the need never arises. Should anything like the demands of that year be brought to the door of the police service in the future it must be hoped that the current structure would be able to repeat the response given at that time. The swinging cuts to budgets, over-necessarily reflected in reductions in patrol constables rather than administrative support, have depleted numbers of those warranted, trained

Summary

and, perhaps also, equipped for such an elongated operation. The always thin blue line seems almost wafer thin today. Perhaps the most evidence of this depletion is reflected in the, previously unheard of, recourse on the part of the Metropolitan Police Service to call for mutual aid from across a large part of southern England to meet the challenges of large-scale street disorder witnessed in 2011, following a police shooting there. The most recent government acknowledgement of the depletion in constable numbers and increased recruitment will assist, but it must be emphasised that experienced officers cannot be brought directly into the service but need to grow their experience to reach the level of performance they must display.

The author hopes that this book has, at least in some part, served to record the view held within the police service, at all levels, during that singularly demanding year. It can, hopefully, be identified as a counter-balance to some other commentaries, too many either politically driven or, too often the modern case, to disguise or confuse where real responsibility rests.

Appendix 1 – Chronology of Events

Particularly in conjunction with the first chapters of this book, it was an interesting exercise to look back at what the press saw as the important moments through this momentous year. The following are chronological and brief extractions from newspapers of the time which focused, of course, upon events directly related to the National Union of Mineworkers Dispute. The rest of the world, although there was considerable international media interest in the Dispute, continued with its unremitting round of the political struggles and natural and man-made disasters that make front page news. Beyond the routine of every-day policing, there were other matters of some greater size for the service in England and Wales to confront alongside this massive operation and some of the more 'newsworthy' are included with this chronology. They are shown in italics.

Date 1984 – 85	Reported Information
12th March	Declaration by the NUM leadership to move from the six-month-long overtime ban, to strike action without a ballot of the members. In a sense the NUM leadership had grabbed

Appendix 1 - Chronology

Date 1984 – 85	Reported Information
	the attention of a media that had, largely, ignored the overtime ban.
15th March	The press reported widely on the violent clashes, especially at Ollerton Colliery in Nottinghamshire, where a picketing striker from Yorkshire died from a chest injury – not attributed to being struck. The figures had been assembled, nationally, and the press reports were that twenty-one of the 174 collieries were working. It was reported that the chairman of the National Coal Board had offered a 5.2% pay rise with the condition that the twenty most uneconomic pits be closed, and that there be a reduction in the workforce of 20,000 through natural wastage. In addition to the recently enacted standing legislation, a High Court injunction was sought against the NUM under the *Employment* Act 1980, which specified the lack of a ballot and the use of flying pickets (the latter a term first used in relation to the NUM in the 1970s) meant that the strike was unlawful.

A View from the Centre

Date 1984 – 85	Reported Information
5th April	The Nottinghamshire miners declared their rejection of the NUM executive's recommendation not to cross picket lines.
9th April	One hundred demonstrators were arrested outside collieries in Nottinghamshire and Derbyshire.
12th April	The president of the NUM vetoes proposals for a national ballot of miners.
17th May	*Police Constable Yvonne Fletcher is shot while assisting in the policing of a demonstration outside the Libyan People's Bureau in London.*
23rd May	First formal talks between the chairman of the NCB and president of the NUM break down after half an hour. The NUM president declares that he will resume discussions only on the pre-condition that there will be no pit closures.
29th May	Forty-one police officers and twenty-eight pickets were injured outside the Orgreave coking plant in South Yorkshire. It was reported that the levels of violence were

Appendix 1 - Chronology

Date 1984 – 85	Reported Information
	influenced by the presence of the NUM president. At Scunthorpe, British Steel workers declared their intention to cross the NUM picket lines.
30th May	The NUM president was arrested for obstruction at Orgreave.
7th June	120 demonstrators were arrested in London after an NUM march from Fleet Street to the Greater London Council building, when about 5,000 marchers broke away across Westminster Bridge to undertake a 'mass lobby' in Parliament Square.
15th June	A Yorkshire striking miner was killed by a lorry outside a power station.
1st August	Legal moves were opened to seize the assets of the South Wales NUM after their refusal to pay fines imposed in relation to the actions in relation to the convoys between Port Talbot and Llanwern.
9th September	The chairman of the NCB attracted much media attention when he arrived for further

A View from the Centre

Date 1984 – 85	Reported Information
	talks with the NUM president in Edinburgh with a paper bag over his head.
12th September	*An Eviction Order was granted against the long-standing encampment of demonstrators around the Greenham Common Air Base.*
21st September	Extreme violence was reported outside Maltby Colliery, near Rotherham.
28th September	The High Court rules the NUM strike to be unlawful.
10th October	The High Court fines the NUM £200,000 and the NUM president £1,000 for contempt.
12th October	*The IRA bomb the Grand Hotel, Brighton, being used by the senior members of the Conservative Party in connection with their annual party conference.*
14th October	The deaths from the Brighton bombing are confirmed at four.
16th October	The pit deputies (safety supervisors), NACODS, vote to go on strike.
24th October	NACODS call off their strike action.

Appendix 1 - Chronology

Date 1984 – 85	Reported Information
5th November	800 formerly striking miners return to work in various areas.
6th November	The High Court freezes £2,700,000 of the assets of the NUM. The order covers £8,700,000 but £6,000,000 had been 'transferred'. The NUM president protests that the strike was in accord with the union's rule forty-one. The Labour Party leader refuses to support the NUM actions.
14th November	The NUM president is fined £250, with £750 costs, for the offence of obstruction on 30th May.
19th November	2,282 more formerly striking miners return to work. This was reported to have brought the current total of miners now working to around 62,000.
20th November	The North Wales branch of the NUM declares an end to strike action.
30th November	Two striking miners are charged with murder of a taxi driver in South Wales.

A View from the Centre

Date 1984 – 85	Reported Information
7th January	Nine striking miners are jailed for arson.
5th February	200 protesters demonstrate outside Molesworth Air Station in Cambridgeshire.
25th February	3,807 more miners are reported returning to work. This was said to bring the total of miners now working to 49% of the total NUM membership.
3rd March	There is a large demonstration outside the Trades' Union Congress headquarters as the NUM executive declares the intention to end the strike, after a vote which was reported as ninety-eight in favour and ninety-one against. The NUM executive agrees that the return to work would be without conditions for an amnesty for those miners dismissed during the dispute. The NUM president denies that the NUM action has suffered a defeat.

Appendix 2 – Collieries

CUMBRIA
Haig

DERBYSHIRE
Arkwright
Bolsover
Cadley Hill
Creswell
High Moor
Ireland
Markham
Renishaw Park
Shirebrook
Westhorpe
Whitewell

DURHAM
Bear Park
Dawdon
Easington
Hawthorn
Horden
Murton
Sacriston
Seaham

Vane Tempest

DYFED POWYS
Betws
Cynheidre
Wernoe

GREATER MANCHESTER
Agecroft
Bickershaw
Golbourne
Parsonage

GWENT
Blaensychan
Brittania
Marine
Markham
Oakdale
North Celynen
Rose Heyworth
Six Bells
South Celynen

KENT
Bettshanger
Snowdon
Tillmanston

LEICESTERSHIRE
Bagworth
Donnisthorpe
Ellis Town
Measham
Nailston
Rawdon
Snibston
South Leicester
Whitwick

MERSEYSIDE
Bold
Crontom
Parkside
Sutton Moor

NORTHUMBRIA
Ashington
Bates
Brenkley
Ellington
Eppleton
Herrington
Lynemouth
Wearmouth
Westow
Whittle

NORTHUMBRIA
Private Mines
Robin Rock Drift
Shadfen
Wrytree Drift

NORTH WALES
Bersham
Point of Ayr

NORTH YORKSHIRE
Gascoine Wood
Kellingley
North Selby
Riccall
Stillingfleet
Whitemoor
Wistoe

NOTTINGHAMSHIRE
Annesley
Babbington
Beavercote
Bentink

Appendix 2 - Collieries

Bilsthorpe
Blidworth
Calverton
Clipstone
Culverhill
Gedling
Harworth
Hucknell
Linby
Mansfield
Moor Green
Newstead
Ollerton
Pye Hill (1)
Pye Hill (2)
Rufford
Sherwood
Sutton
Thoresby
Warsop
Welbeck

SOUTH WALES
Abercanon-Aberdare
Abernant-Cwm Gorse
Aberpergwm Neam
Bedworth-Caerphilly
Blynant-Crynant
Brynlliw-Gorfeinon
Coedely
Cwm-Pontypridd
Deep Navigation-Treharris
Garw Faldau-Maesteg
Lady Windsor-Pontypridd
Mardy-Ton Pentre
Myrther Vale
Nant Gawr-Pontypridd
Penallta-Caerphilly
Penrhiwceiber-Aberdare
St Johns
Taff Merthyr
Tower Aberdare
Treforgan-Crynant
Trelewis-Merthy

SOUTH YORKSHIRE
Askern
Barn Burgh
Barnsley
Bentley
Brodsworth
Brookhouse
Cadeby
Corton Wood
Darfield
Dearne
Dodworth
Elsecar

A View from the Centre

Goldthorpe
Grimethorpe
Hatfield
Hickleton
Highgate
Houghton
Kilnhurst
Kiveton
Maltby
Manvers
Markham
Monkbretton
North Gawber
Orgreave
Redbrook
Rossington
Silverwood
Thorne
Thurcroft

Treeton
Waty Main
Yorkshire

STAFFORDSHIRE

Florence
Hem Heath
Holditch
Lea Hall
Littleton
Silverdale
Worstanton

WARWICKSHIRE

Baddesley
Birch Coppice
Daw Mill
Kerseley

Appendix 4 – Mutual Aid Figures

Appendix 3 – NRC Floor Plan

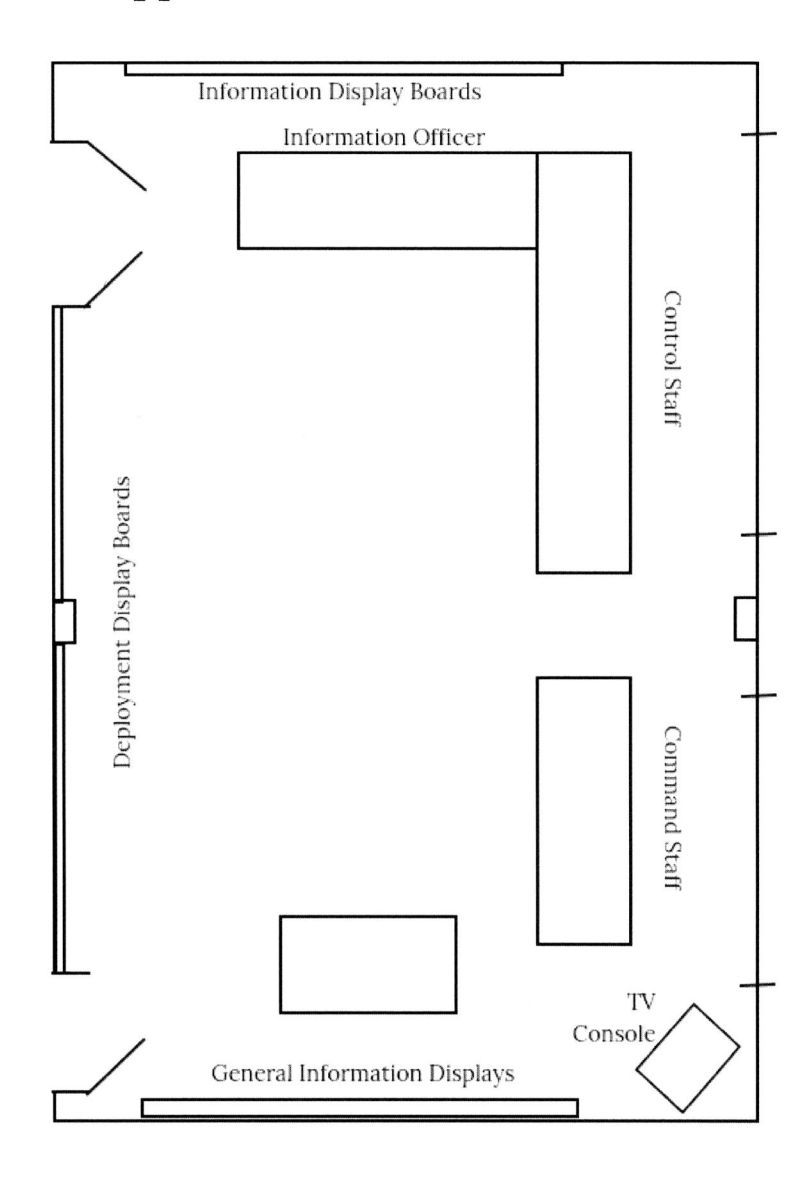

Appendix 4 – Mutual Aid Figures

The figures on the following page are for police support units, the largest aspect of mutual aid from supplying forces, and are shown under the forces to whom they were initially allocated as 'residential aid' or to which they were deployed on a single day basis. Throughout much of the Dispute, there were (sometimes several) re-deployments into other affected force areas. Although these were all recorded at the NRC, the pattern was at times extremely complex, and they are not listed in this appendix.

Many forces chose to send chief inspectors or occasionally superintendents, to another force area, to maintain their own rank structure, where their contingent was of a significant number of PSUs. These officers, with a primarily welfare role, were sometimes supported by Police Federation representative officers and/or representatives from originating forces' welfare departments. The decision to provide these personnel was that of the originating force's chief officer and their cost was not reclaimable nor their deployments treated as one recorded at the NRC.

On a smaller scale but throughout many weeks of the Dispute, there were other forms of mutual aid which are not contained within this appendix. They included superintendents, as colliery commanders; dog handlers and their dogs and mounted officers and their horses.

Appendix 4 – Mutual Aid Figures

The list below is in 'host force' alphabetical order and shows the overall figures for the accumulated days they were allocated, in both PSU's and numbers of officer-days. It must be emphasised that these figures reflect the accumulated days of deployment. Although some of these deployments involved separate tours of duty from home force area, in by far the majority of instances the personnel involved in the colliery areas taking the largest amount of aid were being accommodated throughout the week within those host force areas. The 'day deployment' figures do not totally reflect the extent of the task as, almost invariably, the PSUs and officers were engaged on each working day for longer, not infrequently considerably longer, than the customary eight-hour tour of duty.

A total of twenty-three forces called upon some mutual aid during the fifty-one weeks of the operation of the NRC – just over half of the forces in England and Wales at that time. Some of the smaller and briefer allocations of aid were unconnected with the NUM Dispute but the policy of centralised recording and allocation applied, in order that the NRC fully retained the overall picture. The NRC could only function to its best level when on full activation when all mutual aid was requested through the centre. The non-NUM Dispute related deployments included the policing of nuclear armament protestors in East Anglia and the Conservative Party conference in Brighton, which included the bombing by the IRA of the Grand Hotel. Related deployments well away from colliery areas included the large demonstration mounted in London by the NUM.

A View from the Centre

Although the shifts of greater activity by way of picketing and community violence can be quite closely seen through the deployment requirements received from forces, it must be remembered that there were some forces where local political pressures were exerted upon chief constables to hinder their ability to receive residential aid. This was compensated for by neighbouring chief constables agreeing to accommodate more manpower than they expected to deploy, thus enabling the re-deployments across relatively short distances by the NRC on a day-by-day, sometimes hour-by-hour basis. The early declaration by central government, that the additional expenses incurred would, through a claim system, be recoverable from central funds, enabled this re-deployment process to be operationally highly efficient but without financial loss to those forces where some of their residential mutual aid was being redeployed in significant numbers.

Host Force	PSUs	Officer days	Duration
Cambridgeshire	67	1541	06 – 17/02/84 24/02/84 03/03/85
City of London	22	506	27/09/84
Cleveland	45	1035	02 – 10/07/84
Cumbria	6	138	19/03/84
Derbyshire	10802	248446	18/03 – 22/12/84 01/01 – 06/03/85

Appendix 4 – Mutual Aid Figures

Host Force	PSUs	Officer days	Duration
Durham	1825	41975	14/07/84 24/08 – 02/11/84 08/11 – 22/12/84 01/01 – 06/03/85
Dyfed Powys	10	230	22 – 23/05/84
Essex	6	138	03 – 08/05/84 17/05/84
Gwent	6	138	13/11/84
Humberside	4849	111527	02/04/84 22/05 – 22/12/84
Kent	1656	38088	18 – 19/06/84 19 – 20/07/84 03/09 – 22/12/84 01/01 – 08/03/85
Leicestershire	3345	76935	18/03 – 25/05 03/06 – 22/12/84 01/01 – 03/02/85
Norfolk	2	46	14/06/84
North Wales	305	7015	18/03 – 27/04/84
North Yorkshire	3965	91195	18/06-20/07 16/08 – 22/12/84 01/01 – 06/03/85
Nottinghamshire	18813	432699	14/03 – 22/12/84 01/01 – 02/03/85
South Wales	9	207	05/04 – 08/04/84

A View from the Centre

Host Force	PSUs	Officer days	Duration
South Yorkshire	9338	214774	28/03 – 09/04 12/04; 19/04; 25/05; 29/05 – 22/12/84; 01/01 – 06/03/85
Staffordshire	190	4370	18/03-21/05; 31/05-01/06; 14/08-21/08/84
Suffolk	11	253	23/04/84
Sussex	198	4554	02/09 – 04/09; 07/10 – 12/10/84
Warwickshire	2940	67620	18/03 – 22/12/84; 01/01 – 01/02/85
West Yorkshire	789	18147	11/11 – 22/12/84; 01/01 – 18/01/85
Totals	**59199**	**1361577**	

One PSU = approximately 1 inspector, 2 sergeants & 20 constables (23 officers)

Appendix 5A – Arrests by Police Force Area

The following figures, collated over the fifty-one weeks of the NUM Dispute, were as reported from the respective police force areas. All of these figures were deemed by the reporting forces to have been arrests in connection with the NUM Dispute, although not all were made within colliery areas. In the main, those not in colliery areas were arrests made at demonstrations and in the effort to prevent breaches of the peace at intended picketing destinations.

Police Force Area	Number of Arrests
Cleveland	58
Cumbria	25
Derbyshire	1192
Durham	487
Dyfed Powys	16
Essex	212
Greater Manchester	274
Gwent	236

A View from the Centre

Hampshire	11
Humberside	121
Kent	311
Lancashire	26
Leicestershire	54
Merseyside	195
Metropolitan	255
Northumbria	637
North Wales	31
North Yorkshire	162
Nottinghamshire	2417
South Wales	509
South Yorkshire	1533
Staffordshire	417
Sussex	5
Thames Valley	3
Warwickshire	197
West Yorkshire	425

Appendix 5B – Arrests by Occupation

The following list is in broad categories of occupation of those persons arrested with some identification within the categories where this is thought to be of greater relevance. All those arrested who were members of the NUM are listed within the category 'Miners'.

Category of Occupation	Number Arrested	Examples of Occupation in Category
Miners	8790	
Retired Miners	7	
Unemployed	327	
Manual Workers	273	Construction; Industrial; Local Authority
Students and Academics	105	School & College Students & Lecturers

A View from the Centre

Non-Manual Workers	40	Local Authority; Clerical Staff and Community / Social Workers
Housewives	57	
Transport Workers	18	PSV/HGV drivers & railway workers
Fire Service Workers	10	
Medical Workers	5	Nurses & Hospital Workers
Serviceman	1	Royal Navy
MP/MEP	5	
Justice of the Peace	1	
Retired	2	Non Miners
Females	10	Not specified
Unspecified	156	Occupation not known/given

As was identified in appendix 5A, there is a total error of two in the overall figures for arrests received from source reporting over the fifty-one weeks of the activation of the NRC.

Appendix 5B - Arrests by occupation

As was identified in the introduction, the figures presented in these appendices are composites of information drawn from numerous sources and presented in as succinct a form as has been achievable.

Appendix 5C – Charges Proffered

The following are the charges proffered against arrested and summonsed persons during the NUM Dispute and deemed by reporting forces to be connected with activities relating to the Dispute.

Numbers	Nature of Offence Charged
3	Murder
5	Threats to Kill
2	Unlawful Imprisonment
39	Assault Occasioning Grievous Bodily Harm
430	Assaults Occasioning Actual Bodily Harm
360	Assaults on Police Officers
19	Assault with intent to Resist Arrest
137	Riot
21	Affray
509	Unlawful Assembly
1	Incitement to Riot

Appendix 5C – Charges Proffered

4109	Conduct Likely to Cause a Breach of the Peace (S5 Public Order Act 1936)
207	Breach of the Peace (Common Law)
49	Possession of Offensive Weapon
31	Burglary
275	Besetting (Conspiracy & Protection of Property Act)
13	Threats/Conspiracy to Cause Damage
3	Explosives Offences
4	Criminal Damage with Intent to Endanger Life
15	Arson
1019	Criminal Damage
352	Theft
1	Handling Stolen Property
1	Drug Offence
640	Highway Obstruction
1682	Obstructing a Police Officer in the Execution of His Duty
66	Drunkenness Offences
20	Railway Act Offences (railway trespass)

| 16 | Reckless Driving |
| 32 | Breach of Bail Conditions |

Appendix 5D – Court Results

The court results in this appendix reflect those reported up until the closure of the NRC in March, 1985. At that time there were court cases still in progress which were not, subsequently, collated in the manner that had been undertaken while the NRC was in operation.

Sentence	Numbers	Comments
Imprisonment	160	Longest five years
Detention Centre	37	Longest six months
Youth Custody Order	4	Longest three years
Detained in Police Custody	9	One day each
Attendance Centre	2	
Suspended Sentence	74	Longest six months
Community Order	63	Longest 120 hours
Probation Order	4	
Bound Over to Keep the Peace	1410	

A View from the Centre

Sentence	Numbers	Comments
Conditional/Absolute Discharge	423	
Fines		
Under £10	6	
£10 - £24	185	
£25 - £49	416	
£50 - £74	498	
£75 - £99	587	
£100 - £149	545	
£150 - £199	138	
£200 and above	175	
Total Fined	2550	
Driving Disqualification	1	
Acquittals	1461	

Appendix 6A – Complaints by Police Force

The figures contained in this Appendix are for those areas in which the complaints against the police officers was recorded. No central record was made at the time, or since, regarding the forces from which officers originated. Many complaints received against police officers are more related to the purpose they are pursuing than the individual conduct of the officer. This is true of all complaints against the police not just those reflected in this appendix. Often, when the full situation is appreciated by the member of the public making the complaint, they see why an officer acted in the way that he or she did and withdraw their formal complaint. This, evidently and not exceptionally, applied to about one fifth of the complaints received during the NUM Dispute. To counter-balance the figures for complaints, those for letters of appreciation received in those force areas and relating to the policing of the NUM Dispute are also included.

Police Force Area	Complaints Received	Allegations Withdrawn	Letters of Appreciation
Cheshire	3		
Derbyshire	67	29	173

A View from the Centre

Police Force Area	Complaints Received	Allegations Withdrawn	Letters of Appreciation
Durham	25		7
Dyfed Powys	1		
Essex	1		
Greater Manchester	6	1	17
Gwent	21	1	
Hampshire			4
Humberside	4		33
Kent	20	4	11
Lancashire	4		
Lincolnshire	3	1	1
Merseyside	6		8
Metropolitan	4		
Northumbria	26	1	4
North Wales	2		2
North Yorkshire	1		
Nottinghamshire	62	28	607
South Wales	19		

Appendix 6A – Complaints by Police Force

Police Force Area	Complaints Received	Allegations Withdrawn	Letters of Appreciation
South Yorkshire	241	40	473
Staffordshire	6	3	40
Thames Valley	1		1
Warwickshire	24	4	53
West Yorkshire	6		12

Appendix 6B – Complaints Against Police by Allegation Type

The nature of allegations made by those making complaints against police officers reflect the nature of what was perceived as problematic more than do the force-related figures of the previous appendix. There are, of course, more allegations listed in this appendix than complaints listed in appendix 6A, as some complaints incorporated more than one allegation.

Number	Allegations
257	Assault
117	Incivility
72	Harassment
64	Irregular Procedure
39	Oppressive Conduct
24	Damage to Property
18	Unlawful Arrest
13	Neglect of Duty
9	Motoring Offences

Appendix 7 – Chronology of Intimidation and Violence

The author acknowledges the unidentified compilers of the publication, *The Miners' Dispute. A Catalogue of Violence* of 5th October 1984 and produced by The National Working Miners Committee, Market Place, Ripley, Derbyshire, from which the following schedule of activity during the NUM Dispute 1984 – 85 has been extracted. The introduction to the document acknowledged, accurately, that the information assembled in its pages was nowhere near the full extent of what occurred and it certainly does not reflect more than a small proportion of what was brought to the attention of the NRC. It is used because it was compiled by people who were, or had been until March 1984, members of the NUM and, as such, should be acceptable to the most critical reader of this book as not just the representation as seen by the police.

The *Catalogue* is extensively reflected here as access to an original document seems, now, unlikely.[7] It often names individuals, both injured and culprits and, in some cases, identifies their addresses; but the author has removed these personalised details - where they occurred the substitution is [placed in square brackets]. It is also worthy of comment that

---

[7] Albeit a search for this title online does reveal that someone has recently uploaded an entire scanned version onto the internet.

where estimates of damage are given, it should be remembered that the national average price of a house at the time was in the region of between £25,000 and £30,000. On that note, an interesting report was in the media mid-way through the Dispute, that the NUM President had moved house, into a property costing a reported £120,000!

It has to be identified that the dates of some reported incidents reflect that they were recorded when received and had, in a few instances, occurred the day before. The abbreviations used in the right-hand column are of the sections from the *Catalogue* in which they were recorded, and the information displayed in this manner to provide a chronologically unbroken record. These abbreviations are as follows:

- **WM** = Attacks on working miners and working miners' property
- **P** = Attacks on the police and police property and
- **NCB** = Attacks on National Coal Board staff and property.

Appendix 7 – Chronology of Intimidation and Violence

Date (1984)	Incident Details	Section
Tuesday 13th March	300 flying pickets from Yorkshire forced the closure of a Nottinghamshire pit after fights and scuffles with miners who wanted to continue working. At Bilston Glen many miners who arrived intending to work were intimidated into a hasty about-turn by the prospect of running a gauntlet of about 300 strikers.	WM
Wednesday 14th March	Five arrests were made at Ollerton Colliery as pickets sought to prevent sixty men going in to work.	WM
	A pit manager's car was slightly damaged in scuffles at Hucknall Colliery, near Nottingham.	NCB
Thursday 15th March	The sole working Yorkshire miner conceded defeat after three days' defiance of the pickets. [He], aged fifty-one, went to work at Houghton Main Colliery near Barnsley. Later he found his car over-turned. Its windscreen had been smashed with a lump of concrete.	WM

Date (1984)	Incident Details	Section
	Violence occurred at Ollerton Colliery near Mansfield, Nottinghamshire, where seven police officers were hurt trying to prevent 300 pickets from blockading the main gates as the 450-man dayshift arrived for work. Five pickets were arrested, working miners were punched, and police were pelted with bricks, lumps of wood, milk bottles and fireworks.	P
	At Ollerton Colliery, one lorry window was smashed by a brick and [a passenger] in one of the lorries, had a head injury caused by a missile.	NCB
Saturday 17th March	Two pickets were arrested at Lea Hall Colliery after clashes with local miners. Both were later fined by Rugeley magistrates. One, aged twenty-five, of Doncaster, was fined £300 after admitting using threatening behaviour. His younger brother, aged twenty, of Askern, was fined £150 after admitting obstructing a PC.	WM

Appendix 7 – Chronology of Intimidation and Violence

Date (1984)	Incident Details	Section
Tuesday 20th March	Scuffles took place between miners and police outside the NUM's Barnsley headquarters. Five men were arrested for violent picketing and a police officer was hit by a brick.	P
Saturday 24th March	Five men from South Wales were fined between £100 & £175 each by Stoke-on-Trent magistrates for behaviour likely to cause a breach of the peace at Hem Heath. At Hem Heath working miners found their car windscreens smashed, tyres ripped, and concrete and metal objects strewn in the roads. Pickets had urinated into plastic bags and thrown them at men going into work.	WM
	Between 700 & 800 pickets gathered at Cadley Hill Colliery in South Yorkshire, where ten arrests were made after police officers were injured and three police coaches were damaged.	P
Wednesday 11th April	Police found four-inch nails welded into weapons on the ground on a picket line at Silverdale Colliery, near Stoke-on-Trent, North Staffordshire.	P
Friday 13th April	Cans of fruit rained down on the Nottinghamshire miners' president and two fellow NUM officials.	WM

A View from the Centre

Date (1984)	Incident Details	Section
	A lead-filled bottle cap with four screws sticking out was thrown at a police line. One police officer was injured.	P
Tuesday 17th April	A minor from Grimethorpe Colliery, near Barnsley, who volunteered to work unpaid so that pensioners (retired miners / widows) would receive their coal supplies, found cardboard stuffed in a fuel tank holding forty-five gallons of diesel. It had just caught fire.	WM
	At Sutton Manor on Merseyside the tyres of two vans and a road sweeper were slashed during the night, causing estimated damage of £1,200.	NCB
Thursday 19th April	A miner was punched when he lowered his car window to talk to pickets at Hem Heath Colliery in North Staffordshire. At the same colliery, a working miner's car window was smashed with a brick.	WM
	Several police officers were injured at Wivenhoe Docks as pickets tried to stop coal imports.	P

Appendix 7 – Chronology of Intimidation and Violence

Date (1984)	Incident Details	Section
Saturday 21st April	Angry demonstrators surrounded a delegate when he arrived at Sheffield City Hall for the NUM special delegates conference. They shouted abuse and jabbed fingers into his chest.	WM
Wednesday 2nd May	Nine arrests were made when police stopped miners' cars on the A38 on the Derbyshire border. Stones were thrown at the police.	P
	Seventeen pickets were arrested outside Littleton Colliery, Staffordshire, and the window of a coach taking miners through a picket line at NCB's Trentham Workshops at Stoke-on-Trent was smashed with a crowbar.	NCB
Thursday 3rd May	At Harworth Colliery in north Nottinghamshire, twenty miners were arrested in clashes with police.	P
Friday 4th May	At Cotgrave Colliery, Nottinghamshire eighteen pickets were arrested for throwing stones at working miners.	WM
Saturday 5th May	Nineteen pickets were arrested and one police officer was slightly injured when 2,000 miners laid siege to Hucknall Colliery, north of Nottingham. One charged with causing Actual Bodily Harm or Assault.	P

A View from the Centre

Date (1984)	Incident Details	Section
Tuesday 8th May	Twenty-three men were arrested at Hunterston as pickets tried to prevent a convoy from leaving. Three lorry windscreens were smashed.	NCB
Wednesday 9th May	Five men were arrested and two police officers hurt at Pye Colliery in Nottinghamshire where 2,500 pickets gathered.	P
Thursday 10th May	Police began watch on the house of a Warwickshire miner who received an anonymous note threatening to damage the kidney dialysis machine which keeps his son alive	WM
Monday 26th March	A young miner opposed to the strike was found hanged after being branded a scab. [He], aged twenty-five, was discovered dead by his fiancée, in their flat in County Durham. Her father said that the man had been mercilessly taunted and continually threatened because of his views on the strike.	WM
Tuesday 27th March	Two women Coal Board workers were knocked down and others said they were kicked and spat on when 200 marauding pickets swamped a force of thirty police on guard outside the NCB's Doncaster headquarters.	NCB

Appendix 7 – Chronology of Intimidation and Violence

Date (1984)	Incident Details	Section
Wednesday 28th March	Eight police officers were hurt during scuffles on a picket line outside the NCB area headquarters in Doncaster. One of them, aged twenty-three, collapsed during the scuffles and was taken to hospital. He was later released unhurt. Fifteen miners who clashed with police during the Doncaster picket were later fined a total of £1,550 at Doncaster Magistrates' Court. In all, twenty-two pickets appeared, variously accused of Breach of the Peace, Assault and Criminal Damage.	P
Thursday 29th March	A police officer was dragged along by a car in a go-slow on the M1 on the South Yorkshire - Derbyshire border.	P
Wednesday 4th April	In South Wales, eleven miners were arrested after pickets violently attacked police outside the Port Talbot steelworks.	P
Thursday 5th April	Violence flared at Silverdale Colliery, Newcastle-under-Lyme where pickets smashed windows of cars transporting miners to pits.	WM

Date (1984)	Incident Details	Section
	Women employees were spat on at Stoke-on-Trent Coal Board Offices and a forty-one-year-old man from the finance department was butted in the face by pickets of whom there were 150 in total.	NCB
Friday 6th April	Thirty-nine arrests were made in clashes between pickets and police at Port Talbot steelworks, where 350 men from Nottinghamshire and Northumberland had assembled.	P
Tuesday 10th April	Seventy-eight pickets were arrested and six police officers were hurt outside Creswell and Babbington Collieries in Nottinghamshire..	P
Thursday 10th May	A St John's Ambulance Brigade hut being used by police was burnt down at Gedling Colliery, Nottingham. At Creswell, there were thirteen arrests for criminal damage, public order offences and assaults on police. Twenty police officers were hurt in the scuffles and three required hospital treatment.	P

Appendix 7 – Chronology of Intimidation and Violence

Date (1984)	Incident Details	Section
	Pickets in cars stopped a coach taking women Coal Board staff to work in Duckmanton, north Derbyshire, hurling bricks and stones through the windows, injuring several passengers. Damage to NCB property has also been reported at Oxcroft coal preparation plant in Derbyshire where an 11,000 volt electricity cable carrying the main supply was severed. Office windows were broken in the process. At Pleasley Colliery, north Derbyshire, six heavy plant vehicles were damaged, and sand was poured into the petrol tanks. Windows were broken in offices and outbuildings and the pit was closed following the sabotage. At Langwith Colliery, north Derbyshire, where only surface activity continues, a dumper truck was set on fire.	NCB
Friday 11th May	At Silverdale Colliery in Staffordshire, thirty arrests were made as police endured a barrage of stone throwing.	P

A View from the Centre

Date (1984)	Incident Details	Section
	A coach taking twenty clerical staff to the National Coal Board office in Duckmanton, Derbyshire, was stopped and stoned by pickets and occupants were slightly injured. At Sherwood Colliery in Nottinghamshire, two belts carrying slag from the pithead were slashed.	NCB
Saturday 12th May	Chunks of metal sawn from steel rods were catapulted at working miners at Rufford Colliery in Nottinghamshire.	WM
	Three-inch nails hammered into wood and put inside paper bags were found in roads near Newstead and Annesley Collieries.. Other such nails were concealed in cigarette packets. The motivation behind these tactics was to maim police horses.	P
Tuesday 15th May	Fifty-five men appeared in court facing charges including riot after Monday's mass rally in Mansfield. Eighty-eight arrests were made and forty police officers hurt during the affray.	P

Appendix 7 – Chronology of Intimidation and Violence

Date (1984)	Incident Details	Section
Friday 18th May	Three Yorkshire pickets alleged to have attacked a Nottinghamshire miner on his way to work were charged with intimidation under the *Conspiracy and Protection Act* at Mansfield magistrates' court.	WM
Tuesday 22nd May	Two police officers were slightly injured when a concrete block was thrown through a window of their van near Rufford Colliery, Mansfield.	P
Friday 25th May	At Welbeck Colliery, north Nottinghamshire, forty-five men were arrested. Five miners tried to pass 150 pickets. Fights then broke out and two police officers were injured.	P
Wednesday 30th May	Eighty-four people were arrested and sixty-four injured at Orgreave. Stones, wooden fencing, a shovel, and a bucket were thrown at police. They were also bombarded with smoke bombs and one officer sustained a broken leg.	P

Date (1984)	Incident Details	Section
Thursday 31st May	At Orgreave, miners had left a telegraph pole, a battering ram, barbed wire and a burning Portakabin across the road in order to frustrate the police. Thirty-five pickets were arrested and sixteen police injured. A police horse cut its leg. Three miners were arrested outside a NCB office and a police officer was injured.	P
Friday 1st June	At Orgreave, ten arrests were made and one police officer was injured in violent clashes.	P
Saturday 2nd June	Nineteen men were arrested at Orgreave and twenty injured, including five police. According to police chief, "Six officers were given a good hiding".	P
Thursday 7th June	Violence flared at Orgreave where twenty-three were arrested. Eight police officers were hurt and three burnt by paint stripper.	P

Appendix 7 – Chronology of Intimidation and Violence

Date (1984)	Incident Details	Section
	Seven pit-top conveyor belts were cut through during the night at Silverdale Colliery. Production was unaffected. Damage was put at around £5,000. Damage of over £10,000 was caused to machinery and telephone wires at a private open cast mine in Lanarkshire.	NCB
Friday 8th June	120 arrests were made on the miners' march through London. Two police officers were injured, and a woman was knocked down and trampled.	P
Friday 15th June	Striking miner was convicted of obstructing a police officer at a picket line at Tow Law. He was fined £50 and ordered to pay £50 costs.	P
Sunday 17th June	The windows of two buses and a car were broken following an ambush by pickets as miners at Shirebrook drove into work. Seven arrests were made, and two police officers were hurt.	WM
Monday 18th June	At Maltby, near Rotherham, twenty-nine arrests were made and one police officer had a suspected broken nose.	P

Date (1984)	Incident Details	Section
Tuesday 19th June (actually 18th)	At Orgreave, eighty were hurt and one hundred arrested following horrifying scenes at the coking plant. Stones, bottles, bricks, iron bars and jagged glass were thrown at police. Pickets set up a barricade of burning cars, lamp posts and of stones from a wall they had demolished. Wooden stakes had also been planted in the ground. There were twenty-one arrests at Shirebrook colliery, north Derbyshire, after clashes between police and 450 pickets.	P
Wednesday 20th June	Following incidents at Orgreave on 18th June, twenty-four were charged with rioting.	P
Thursday 21st June	Working miner committed suicide after his twelve-year-old daughter was threatened with violence by pickets.	WM

Appendix 7 – Chronology of Intimidation and Violence

Date (1984)	Incident Details	Section
Wednesday 27th June	At the NCB regional offices in Doncaster, thirty-seven people, nineteen of them women, were assaulted, hit by stones or otherwise threatened. One girl was taken to hospital after being punched in the mouth and another was told that she would be "kicked back home" if she went into work. One man was spat on as he approached the office.	NCB
Tuesday 3rd July	At Shirebrook colliery, six were arrested for obstruction and five police officers were injured.	P
Friday 6th July	Two clerical staff at Shirebrook colliery were stoned and abused.	NCB
Saturday 7th July	At Selby, North Yorkshire, violent scenes developed as pickets occupied a toll (weigh) bridge. Ten police officers were injured. Three miners were arrested as police vehicles were over-turned at Whitemore.	P

Date (1984)	Incident Details	Section
Tuesday 10th July	Thirteen terrified NCB managers and maintenance staff were rescued by police after being held siege in a pit for eleven hours. Windows were smashed and other property damaged. Four more South Wales haulage firms involved in convoys maintaining coal and iron ore supplies to Llanwern have been attacked. Thirteen lorries were damaged, paint was sprayed on windscreens and sugar was poured into fuel tanks.	NCB
Wednesday 11th July	Stones were thrown and windows broken at Hemsworth police station. West Yorkshire. At Fitzwilliam pub nearby, officers were avalanched by stones and missiles.	P
	£100,000 damage was done to a drift mine near Llanwern and many vehicles were set on fire.	NCB
Wednesday 25th July	At Port Talbot, where 500 pickets assembled, five lorries had their windows smashed by missiles. Thirty-four people were arrested, including seven women.	NCB

Appendix 7 – Chronology of Intimidation and Violence

Date (1984)	Incident Details	Section
Friday 27th July	At Bilston Glen, fifty-two arrests were made after a 300 strong picket failed to prevent twenty-two men from going to work. Some of the strikers tore down fencing and started a bonfire but the most serious incident involved the arrest of forty pickets who surrounded the nearby home of a working miner.	WM
Saturday 28th July	The first picket to be arrested at Bilston Glen was fined £500 for a Breach of the Peace. A twenty-one–year-old, aimed a punch at an eighteen year old miner's craft apprentice opposed to the strike.	WM
	At South Shields, Tyne and Wear, pickets occupied NCB workshops and chained the gates. Thirty arrests were made.	NCB

Date (1984)	Incident Details	Section
Tuesday 31st July	Six articulated lorries which had been moving coal from Nottinghamshire pits to power stations were destroyed by arson, causing £200,000 damage. The vehicles belonged to a Midlands haulage company. Three other lorries were damaged. They were owned by a bulk transport company of Ashfield, Nottinghamshire and parked at the rear of the company's depot.	NCB
Saturday 4th August	About 200 miner pickets vandalised a Coal Board transport depot in Derbyshire. Fourteen lorries and two coaches at the South Normanton depot had windows smashed and bodies dented. Damage was estimated at £4,000.	NCB
Tuesday 7th August	Ten vehicles used for hauling coal in the Derbyshire / Nottinghamshire coalfield were found damaged.	NCB

Appendix 7 – Chronology of Intimidation and Violence

Date (1984)	Incident Details	Section
Wednesday 8th August	At Birch Copice Colliery in Warwickshire, stones were thrown at working miners' coaches as they approached the pithead. Two arrests were made. In Cumbria, twenty-three pickets from the North-East of England were interviewed by police after lorry drivers were attacked and injured at a coal loading point at Maryport. Two lorry drivers were taken to hospital and five men charged with criminal damage and assault. The brake pipes of a car belonging to a working miner from Hucknall colliery, Nottinghamshire were severed. Bricks and paint were indiscriminately hurled at overseers as they reported for their shift.	WM
	In the North-East, ten men were arrested when 600 pickets tried to stop thirty white-collar union members reporting for duty at NCB stores at Philadelphia, near Sunderland. Between fifty- and sixty-men stoned NCB offices in Doncaster. Fifteen windows were smashed and three people arrested.	NCB

Date (1984)	Incident Details	Section
Thursday 9th August	There were violent scenes at Harworth colliery when about 1,000 demonstrators gathered at noon and attacked working miners who were arriving for the afternoon shift. A group of twenty striking miners attacked a shopkeeper standing outside a wine bar in Rugeley, Staffordshire. They then entered and beat up a young working miner inside.	WM
	Five Northumberland miners received suspended sentences of between three- and nine-months for an attack they made with a pickaxe handle and a sledgehammer on a fleet of lorries. Ninety-five people were arrested in Nottinghamshire as a public bus was stoned. A privately-owned open cast mine at Westerhope / Westerthorpe, near Newcastle-upon-Tyne suffered £7,000 damage after a sabotage raid.	NCB

Appendix 7 – Chronology of Intimidation and Violence

Date (1984)	Incident Details	Section
Friday 10th August	[A miner], aged fifty-four, went to work at Garw Colliery, South Wales. He was pelted with eggs, bricks and bottles by over 300 strikers, their wives and children. Seven arrests were made, and police were only able to escort him home three hours after the end of his shift. The Nottinghamshire area of the Coal Board reported £150,000 worth of criminal damage. In addition, £40,000 worth of damage was caused to 422 vehicles, mostly belonging to working miners. Cars had windscreens smashed, headlights kicked in and bodywork attacked. Dirt had been poured into fuel tanks and brake pipes were found severed.	WM
Saturday 11th August	A £3,000 sports car owned by a working miner was destroyed in an arson attack outside the man's home in Laneham, near Retford, Nottinghamshire. Police examined the vehicle and found a candle stuck to a piece of petrol-soaked sacking near the foot pedals.	WM

Date (1984)	Incident Details	Section
Monday 13th August	Police are treating as arson a fire at an engineering works at Pleasley Vale, north Derbyshire, in which five coaches belonging to the National Coal Board were destroyed after an inflammable liquid was thrown over them. An office block was also attacked and the total cost of the damage caused was £30,000.	NCB
Tuesday 14th August	At Cuckney, three miles from Welbeck Colliery in Nottinghamshire, 2,000 pickets clashed with police. As police stopped cars at a roadblock, pickets hurled bricks and stones at police. Two officers were injured.	P
Friday 17th August	The pregnant wife of a Staffordshire working miner collapsed with shock after a piece of concrete was thrown through a window at their home and landed in a cot. [The woman], aged twenty-three, of Rugeley, was expecting twins the following month. She and her husband found the concrete in a nursery that they had prepared.	WM

Appendix 7 – Chronology of Intimidation and Violence

Date (1984)	Incident Details	Section
	In scuffles at Gascoigne Wood one police officer had his nose broken and there were five arrests. Pickets set fire to rolls of straw dragged from a field nearby into the Colliery approach road. As they dispersed, they stoned two police coaches, shattering windows, and knocked a police motorcyclist off his machine.	P
	A twenty-five-year-old miner appeared before magistrates at Stoke-on-Trent. He was alleged to have destroyed and damaged by fire three coaches and a van in an alleged arson attack on a vehicle park in Trentham early yesterday. He was remanded in custody for four days.	NCB
Saturday 18th August	There was violence at Gascoigne Wood. Bricks and clods of earth were thrown at police.	P

Date (1984)	Incident Details	Section
Tuesday 21st August	[A man] who lives at Thurcroft, near Rotherham, South Yorkshire and works at Bevercotes Colliery, Nottinghamshire, had a brick hurled through his window on 6th July. Ten striking miners paid fines and compensation to him totalling £2,135 after admitting threatening behaviour and actual damage.	WM
	At Selston, near Mansfield, Nottinghamshire, a brick was hurled through the windscreen of a moving police car.	P
	A former Coal Board worker who punched and kicked a police sergeant was jailed for twenty-one days. [He] was aged thirty-two of Keresley, Warwickshire.	P

Appendix 7 – Chronology of Intimidation and Violence

Date (1984)	Incident Details	Section
	Six striking miners accused of arson were remanded in custody by Stoke-on-Trent magistrates. The men, from Hem Heath pit, are alleged to have destroyed and damaged by fire two AEC coaches, one Ford coach and one Leyland minivan worth a total of £130,000. A striking north Derbyshire miner who carried out a sabotage attack on a Coal Board depot was jailed for nine months by a Derbyshire court. [He], aged forty-three, from Markham colliery, admitted cutting through an 11,000 volt cable.	NCB
Wednesday 22nd August	At Silverwood colliery, near Rotherham, almost 1,000 pickets mustered before dawn to try to prevent a lone worker, an electrician aged fifty-four, from going to work. , They burnt scrap cars, trees and supermarket trolleys in the road and launched a barrage of bricks and stones at police. Eight police officers were hurt.	P

A View from the Centre

Date (1984)	Incident Details	Section
	There were ugly scenes at Hatfield, near Doncaster,, where pickets set up a barricade of trees and set an old car on fire on a road close to the colliery. A police car had its windows smashed by stones in a neighbouring village.	P
Thursday 23rd August	Police are investigating five instances of windows being broken at the homes of working miners in north Derbyshire. A miner at Eckington had all four tyres on his car slashed and another miner on his way to Shirebrook colliery, Derbyshire, had his car damaged by a picket wielding an iron bar.	WM

Appendix 7 – Chronology of Intimidation and Violence

Date (1984)	Incident Details	Section
	Senior police officers admitted that they were deeply concerned at the emergence of a paramilitary style gang, apparently led by a woman, which spearheaded a day of unprecedented violence in Yorkshire pit villages. They were dressed in camouflage jackets, boiler suits and balaclava helmets. Police tackled pickets in villages surrounding the pits of Bentley, Markham Main and Yorkshire Main after barricades were erected and set on fire, pit stores looted, and equipment wrecked. At Bentley, fifty people led by a woman were spotted, uniformed, in the pit yard. They attacked spy cameras and stole donkey jackets and pickaxe handles.	P
	The office of a County Durham taxi firm used by the National Coal Board to take men into work was attacked. A window was broken, a telephone pulled out and a minibus vandalised.	NCB

A View from the Centre

Date (1984)	Incident Details	Section
Friday 24th August	A twenty-seven-year-old strike official of Dunfermline was fined £250 and ordered to pay £100 compensation at Dunfermline sheriff court after he admitted assaulting a miner who went back to work.	WM
	Forensic scientists examined three suspected petrol bombs found by police after they had clashed with pickets in a Yorkshire pit village. They were discovered in the garden of a house in Armthorpe, near Doncaster, after running battles outside Markham colliery.	P
Saturday 25th August	After a man returned to work, hundreds of miners went to Easington colliery to protest. Police said that the men "ran riot. Office staff were forced to shelter in corridors as bricks smashed windows sending glass flying and the 500-strong pickets rampaged through the colliery car park. Six cars were damaged, including that of the colliery manager. An Audi was overturned. Five police officers were injured, and four pickets arrested.	NCB

Appendix 7 – Chronology of Intimidation and Violence

Date (1984)	Incident Details	Section
Wednesday 29th August	A Polish born miner who has been off work for twelve months discovered his house daubed with swastikas and graffiti. [He], who worked at Silverdale colliery near Newcastle-under-Lyme, has a son employed at the pit.	WM
	A cable was strung at neck height across a public road. A working miner hit the cable and was catapulted off his motorcycle as he returned home from Renishaw Park colliery.	WM
Thursday 30th August	Eighty-seven strikers were arrested in Scotland when pickets congregated around the home of a working miner in the village of New Cumrock in the Ayrshire coalfield.	WM

A View from the Centre

Date (1984)	Incident Details	Section
Friday 31st August	Three men are being questioned by police after a petrol bomb attack on a car belonging to a miner who had returned to work after being on strike. Petrol bombs were thrown at the car but bounced off the bonnet, exploded and caused slight damage. Three men wearing combat clothing and balaclavas were seen running away from the home of a working miner, aged eighteen, of Warsop near Mansfield, Nottinghamshire.	WM
	A man went to work at Easington. Arrests were made and several police hurt when pickets charged.	P
	Two arrests were made in north Derbyshire when some pickets stoned a Coal Board bus.	NCB
Saturday 1st September	A police horse was stoned to the ground and injured, and three police officers had glass showered in their eyes when their coach was attacked in the worst violence so far at Kiverton Park colliery in South Yorkshire. Windscreens were shattered together with two large windows of a Metropolitan Police coach as it was pelted with rocks.	P

Appendix 7 – Chronology of Intimidation and Violence

Date (1984)	Incident Details	Section
Wednesday 5th September	Fifteen striking miners were being questioned by Derbyshire Police last night about attacks on homes and other property of working miners. Police in Derbyshire investigating a report that two children, aged six and eight, of striking miners at Shirebrook Colliery were approached in the street and told not to play with children of working miners. A lighted rag was pushed through the letter-box of a working miner in Shirebrook.	WM
	A striking miner who threatened the children of a working colleague was ordered to do 150 hours of unpaid work for the community at Edinburgh sheriff court yesterday. [The man], aged twenty-four, of Dalkeith, had shouted at the miner, "Your bairns will get it at the school. They will get their guts cut out. We can do anything we like and get away with it."	WM

Date (1984)	Incident Details	Section
Thursday 6th September	Twelve striking miners from north Derbyshire were remanded in custody yesterday after appearing in court in Chesterfield on charges of Riotous Assembly in connection with an alleged attack on working miners in the county last week.	WM
	A maintenance worker at Betteshanger Colliery, Kent, was attacked and injured by striking miners when he emerged from the pit entrance to talk to pickets. He was taken to hospital and later released.	WM

Appendix 7 – Chronology of Intimidation and Violence

Date (1984)	Incident Details	Section
Friday 7th September	Thirteen people, including a policeman, were hurt at Kellingley colliery, North Yorkshire, where 4,000 pickets gathered. Police were showered with broken glass and pieces of concrete outside the pit, known as 'Big K', where two men were working. An ITN car was over-turned and set on fire. £10,000 worth of camera equipment was stolen. Twenty-four men from Barnsley and Rotherham areas appeared before Selby magistrates on public order offences. They were remanded on bail for a week. Two policemen are now in Pontefract Infirmary with rib and head injuries.	P
Tuesday 11th September	An array of weapons used by miners' pickets was put on show by police. Included were a heavy chain, ball-bearings and booby traps designed to maim men, horses, and dogs.	P

Date (1984)	Incident Details	Section
	Two pickets who covered a road with spiked belts to stop police escorting a miner to work were fined £750 each at Dunfermline sheriff court. [The two men were named], one twenty-nine-years-old, and one thirty-five, of Dunfermline.	P
	Thirty-five men appeared in court at Chesterfield charged with Unlawful Assembly in connection with an incident in which £1,000 damage was caused to a Coal Board van and a police car near Whitwell colliery, north Derbyshire last week.	NCB
Saturday 20th September	Two striking miners were arrested and kept in custody for thirty-two hours after making a bogus 999 call to report a traffic accident. The men, father and son, aged forty-six & twenty-three, were charged with threatening behaviour, possessing a pickaxe handle as an offensive weapon and attempting to beset a place of employment, namely Bolsover colliery.	NCB

Appendix 7 – Chronology of Intimidation and Violence

Date (1984)	Incident Details	Section
Monday 22nd September	[A man], of Mansfield Woodhouse, and a surface engineer at Shirebrook colliery, said that there had been up to 2,500 pickets at his pit. Bricks had been thrown, hay bales set alight, and attempts made to push the police under vehicles taking miners to work. The man stopped going to work for a period after finding three men outside his house who told him, "We will not stop you going to work but bear in mind you have got a wife and kids in there." He had frequently received threatening calls throughout the night and the word scab had been daubed on his car.	WM
	A quality control inspector from Markham colliery said that his car had been stoned, oil poured on his road, a ball-bearing hurled at his window and that another vehicle had swerved in a deliberate attempt to overturn his own car.	WM

Date (1984)	Incident Details	Section
Wednesday 26th September	Miners' pickets in South Wales yesterday ambushed a 140 strong convoy of heavy lorries ferrying coal and iron ore fifty miles along the M4 from Port Talbot to Llanwern Steelworks. Ten vehicles were damaged. Police produced a 4ft wooden pit prop as one of the missiles hurled. Windscreens were smashed and a large stone crashed through one lorry's glass-fibre roof.	NCB
Friday 28th September	A Staffordshire NUM official, twenty-nine-years, appeared at Fenton magistrates in Stoke-on-Trent charged with assaulting a working miner and damaging his car. The hearing was adjourned until 3rd October.	WM
Saturday 29th September	A striking miner who set fire to a coach being used to ferry working miners to Bickershaw colliery at Leigh, Lancashire, was given a jail sentence at Bolton crown court. [He] aged thirty-seven, was sentenced to nine months imprisonment, six months of which were suspended. He admitted arson.	WM

Appendix 7 – Chronology of Intimidation and Violence

Date (1984)	Incident Details	Section
Tuesday 2nd October	A working miner from Manton colliery, Yorkshire was subject to an attempt to run his car off the road. He was driving near Worksop, Nottinghamshire with his wife and children, when a car containing five striking miners pulled alongside and forced his car off the road. They made death threats against him and his family and specifically threatened to kill his children.	WM

Index

1829, v, 4, 5
1911, 6, 28, 47
1968, 6
1972, v, 7
1974, 6, 8
  April, 62
1978, v, 1, 21
1979, 1, 2
  May, 1, 2
1980, i, 2, 3, 8, 15, 42, 50, 78, 84
  April, 2
1981, 2, 3, 8, 11, 12, 20, 42, 50, 78, 81
  April, 2, 11
  July, 2, 11
1982, 3, 8, 78
1983, i, ii, 1, 9, 13, 42, 62, 78
  September, 13
1984, 3, iii, iv, v, vi, vii, ix, 6, 8, 9, 11, 12, 13, 14, 15, 16, 17, 21, 24, 26, 29, 31, 33, 37, 38, 40, 41, 47, 59, 62, 76, 78, 81
  April, 57, 85, 118
  August, 57, 86, 133
  July, 130
  June, 53, 55, 86, 127
  March, 9, 13, 14, 15, 17, 21, 22, 24, 26, 83, 114, 116
  May, 85, 120
  November, 58, 88

  October, 58, 64, 70, 71, 74, 87, 114
  September, 86, 145
1985, 3, ii, iii, vii, 1, 34, 41, 59, 76, 81
  February, 89
  January, 41, 89
  March, 75, 77, 89, 108
  September, 80
1987, 81
2011, 82
Association of Chief Police Officers, i, ii, vii, 3, 4, 7, 10, 12, 13, 14, 15, 19, 21, 22, 29, 30, 33, 34, 35, 36, 38, 39, 41, 75, 76, 79, 80
  conference, 80
  debrief, 80
  General Purposes Committee, 4, 13, 33, 78
  president of, i, ii, 7, 12, 13, 14, 15, 19, 21, 22, 29, 34, 36, 38, 39, 41, 47, 75, 85
  Public Order Sub-Committee, 4, 78
Avon and Somerset Constabulary, 15, 28, 41
BBC, 31
Birmingham, 2, 53
Blockade, 53
Boyer, Robert, 59

Index

Bristol, i, 15
  St. Paul's, 2, 3
British Steel, 86
Brittan, Sir Leon. *See* Home Secretary
Broome, Ronald, 41
Cambridgeshire, 89
Cambridgeshire Police, 35, 37, 40, 97
Cheshire Constabulary, 110
Chief Constables, 2, 3, 5, 6, 7, 13, 14, 15, 18, 21, 23, 24, 27, 28, 29, 30, 33, 35, 41, 53, 64, 78, 97
  autonomy of, 21, 29, 47
  Broome, Ronald, 41
  East, David, 27
  Hall, David, 13
  MacLachlan, Charles, 14, 17, 18, 21, 22, 41
  Wright, Peter, 54
Churchill, Winston, 47
City of London Police, 6, 13, 97
Clement, Tony, 54
Cleveland Constabulary, 97, 100
Coal
  import of, 52, 119
  production, 52
  stockpiling of, 52
  transport of, 28, 52, 56, 58, 131, 133, 151
Coal Mining Industry
  collieries open, 84

demise of, iv
nationalisation of, 68
subsidisation of, 62, 68, 84
subsidising of, 69
Collieries, 90, *See* Appendix 2 *passim.*
  Annesley, 125
  Babbington, 91, 123
  Bentley, 92, 142
  Betteshanger, 147
  Bevercotes, 139
  Bilston Glen, 116, 132
  Birch Copice, 134
  Bolsover, 149
  Cadley Hill, 90, 118
  Cotgrave, 120
  Creswell, 90, 123
  Easington, 143, 145
  Garw, 92, 136
  Gascoigne Wood, 138
  Gedling, 123
  Grimethorpe, 119
  Harworth, 135
  Harworth Colliery, 120
  Hatfield, 141
  Hem Heath, 118, 119, 140
  Houghton Main, 116
  Hucknall, 116, 120, 134
  Kellingley, 148
  Kiverton Park, 145
  Langwith, 124
  Lea Hall, 117
  Littleton, 93, 120
  Maltby, 87
  Manton, 152

Markham, 140, 143, 150
Markham Main, 142
Newstead, 125
Ollerton, 116, 117
Pleasley, 124
police commanders, 65, 95
Pye, 92, 121
remaining open, 84
Renishaw Park, 90, 144
Rufford, 92, 125, 126
Sherwood, 19, 20, 92, 125
Shirebrook, 90, 128, 129, 130, 141, 146, 150
Silverdale, 93, 118, 122, 124, 128, 144
Silverwood, 140
Welbeck, 92, 126, 137
Whitwell, 149
Yorkshire Main, 142
Community
  impact on, 48, 50, 56, 58, 67, 68
  policing of, 56, 59, 64, 66, 68
  spirit, 67
Conservative Party, 2, 9, 57
  conference, 57, 64, 87, 96
  conference bombing, 57, 87, 96
Conspiracy and Protection Act, 126
Constables
  Crown Servants, 81

injured, 72, 85, 117, 118, 119, 122, 123, 125, 126, 127, 128, 130, 137, 138, 139, 140, 143, 145, 148
killed, 85
loss of, 81
overtime payment, 65, 66, 67
powers of, 5, 6
roles in NRC, 14
County & Borough Police Act 1856, 5
County Durham, 121
County Police Act 1839, 4
Crimes
  arson, 89, 131, 133, 136, 137, 138, 140, 141, 145, 146, 148, 151
  assault, 117, 120, 122, 123, 124, 132, 134, 135, 143, 151
  assault police, 72, 85, 117, 118, 119, 122, 123, 127, 138, 139, 148, 150
  by police officers, 113
  charges for. *See* Appendix 5c *passim*.
  criminal damage, 116, 118, 119, 120, 121, 122, 123, 124, 125, 128, 131, 133, 134, 135, 136, 139, 141, 142, 143, 144, 149, 150, 151
  murder, 58, 59, 72, 85, 88
  obstruction, 86, 117, 128
  persons arrested for, 72, 75, 85, 86, 100, 102, 103,

Index

105, 116, 117, 118, 120, 121, 122, 123, 124, 125, 126, 127, 128, 129, 130, 131, 132, 134, 135, 136, 138, 143, 144, 145, 149, *See* Appendices 5A and 5B *passim.*
  reporting of, 48
  riot, 125, 129, 147
  theft, 142, 148
Cumbria, 24, 100, 134
Cumbria Police, 97
Derbyshire, 24, 76, 85, 114, 120, 122, 133, 140, 141, 145, 147
  Bolsover colliery, 149
  Chesterfield, 149
  Duckmanton, 124, 125
  Langwith colliery, 124
  Markham colliery, 143
  miners allegiances, 57
  Oxcroft coal preparation plant, 124
  Pleasley, 137
  Pleasley colliery, 124
  Renishaw Park colliery, 144
  Ripley, 71
  Shirebrook colliery, 128, 129, 130, 141, 146, 150
  Whitwell colliery, 149
Derbyshire Constabulary, 24, 97, 100, 110, 146
Durham, 142

Durham Constabulary, 98, 100, 111
Dyfed Powys Police, 28, 98, 100, 111
East, David, 27
Energy Ministry, 22
  preparations for NUM Dispute, 52
Essex Police, 98, 100, 111
Falkland Islands, 3
Fletcher, Yvonne, 85
Frogson, Keith, 59
Gloucestershire Constabulary, 28
Government
  boundary changes, 62
  funding, 63
  interference with policing, viii, 21, 29, 30, 37, 47, 63, 70, 82, 97
  overthrow of, iv, 1, 2, 53, 55, 58, 69, 70
  resistance to pressure, v, 63
  responses to Miner's strike, iv
Greater Manchester Police, 100, 111
Greenham Common Air Base, 87
Gwent
  Llanwern, 86, 131, 151
Gwent Police, 28, 98, 100, 111
Hall, David, 13, 34, 36

Hampshire Constabulary, 44, 76, 101, 111
High Court, 84, 87, 88
Home Office, 8, 14, 18, 19, 21, 35, 39
Home Secretary, 39, 47, 63, 75
   Brittan, Sir Leon, 63
   Churchill, Winston, 47
Humberside, 13, 28, 58
   Immingham, 52
   Scunthorpe, 86
Humberside Police, 13, 28, 98, 101, 111
Independent Television News, 31, 148
Information. *See* Intelligence
Intelligence
   sources of, 31, 36, 38, 70
Intimidation. *See* Appendix 7 *passim.*
   of families, 49, 50, 56, 58, 67, 68, 72, 74, 121, 129, 137, 146, 150, 152
   striking miners to working miners, 22, 48, 55, 56, 58, 67, 69, 71, 72, 73, 116, 121, 126, 132, 134, 140, 141, 144, 145, 146, 149, 150
IRA. *See* Irish Republicanism
Irish Republicanism, 3, 57, 87, 96
Justices of the Peace. *See* Magistrates
Kent, 53

Betteshanger colliery, 147
Kent Police, 98, 101, 111
Labour Party, 88
Lanarkshire, 128
Lancashire Constabulary, 101, 111, 151
Leeds, 2
Leicestershire, 24
Leicestershire Police, 24, 98, 101
Lincolnshire Police, 111
Liverpool
   Toxteth, 2
London, 2, 5, 6, 13, 14, 22, 29, 31, 33, 35, 41, 47, 85, 86, 96, 128
   Brixton, 2
MacLachlan, Charles, 21, 22, 41
Magistrates, 5, 103, 117, 118, 126, 138, 140, 148, 151
Manchester, 2
Merseyside, 119
Merseyside Police, 101, 111
Metropolitan Police, ii, v, 4, 7, 13, 14, 15, 18, 19, 20, 22, 26, 34, 36, 38, 40, 41, 78, 82, 101, 111, 145
   Hendon training school, 34
   New Scotland Yard, ii, 4, 7, 11, 12, 15, 29, 38, 39, 53, 78, 80
Miners Strike
   arrests, 72

Index

cost of, 62, 73
intent to end, 89
legality of, 84, 87
negotiations to avoid, 84, 85, 87
political intentions, 49, 69, 72
stated aim of, 77
Molesworth Air Station, 89
Municipal Corporations Act 1836, 4
Mutual Aid, 6, 7, 8, 9, 17, 19, 24, 26, 28, 30, 32, 35, 36, 39, 41, 42, 44, 48, 53, 62, 63, 64, 65, 66, 95, 96, 97, *See* Appendix 4 *passim*.
   accommodation of, 24, 27, 28, 30, 43, 67, 95, 96, 97
   arrangement of, 25, 62, 64, 80
   communications, 80
   historical examples, 6, 7, 8
   issues in Wales, 28, 52
   largest deployment of, 53
   monitoring of, 11
   of superintending ranks, 34, 41, 95
   payment for, 27, 31, 62, 63, 64, 95, 97
   redeployment of, 30, 32, 95, 97
   requesting, 14, 17, 18, 19, 22, 23, 24, 53, 82, 96
   specialist roles, 41, 53, 54, 67, 95

Mutual Aid Coordination Centre, iv, 80, 81, *See*, *See* National Reporting Centre
National Coal Board, 9, 71, 73, 85, 86, 115, 116, 117, 119, 120, 121, 123, 124, 125, 127, 128, 130, 131, 132, 133, 134, 135, 136, 137, 138, 139, 140, 142, 143, 145, 149, 151
   collieries open, 84
   headquarters, 121, 122
   pay offer, 84
   Trentham Workshops, 120
National Police Coordination Centre, iv, *See* National Reporting Centre
National Reporting Centre, i, ii, iii, iv, vii, 7, 8, 9, 11, 12, 13, 14, 15, 16, 17, 18, 19, 20, 21, 22, 24, 25, 26, 28, 29, 30, 31, 32, 33, 34, 35, 36, 37, 38, 39, 40, 41, 44, 53, 55, 57, 70, 71, 75, 76, 78, 79, 80, 81, 95, 96, 97, 103, 108, 114, *See*
   command structure, 16, 35, 40
   communications, 12, 17, 18, 20, 32, 36, 37, 38
   establishment of, 7, 11, 78
   layout of, 94
   methods of working, 20, 35, 37, 40
   reports, 75

reports from, 21, 29, 37, 38, 39
shift pattern, 15, 22, 29, 38, 39, 41, 81
staff officers, 14, 19, 21, 22, 29, 31, 32, 33, 34, 35, 36, 37, 38, 39, 41, 53
technology, 36, 38
test exercise, 79
National Union of Mineworkers, 3, i, iii, iv, vi, ix, x, 8, 9, 10, 11, 13, 14, 18, 23, 30, 31, 34, 35, 39, 40, 47, 49, 52, 53, 54, 55, 56, 57, 59, 62, 65, 66, 67, 68, 69, 76, 77, 79, 80, 85, 86, 87, 88, 89, 96, 102, 110, 114, 118, 120, 151
court verdict, 86, 87, 88
Dispute, iii, iv, vi, ix, x, 8, 9, 10, 34, 35, 39, 40, 49, 57, 59, 62, 65, 66, 67, 76, 79, 80, 81, 83, 96, 100, 105, 110, 114
headquarters, 118
injunction, 84
leadership, 9, 10, 13, 14, 18, 47, 49, 51, 53, 54, 55, 69, 72, 73, 83, 85, 86, 87, 88, 89, 115
overtime ban, 9, 10, 13, 14, 23, 52, 79, 83
political aims. *See* Government: overthrow of

National Working Miners Committee, 70, 71, 72, 74, 76, 114
Aims, 72
publication
The Miners' Dispute. A Catalogue of Violence. *See* The Miners' Dispute. A Catalogue of Violence
Norfolk Constabulary, 19, 98
North Wales, 24, 88
miners allegiances, 57
North Wales Police, 24, 98, 101, 111
North Yorkshire, 130
Gascoigne Wood colliery, 138
Kellingley colliery, 148
North Yorkshire Police, 98, 101, 111
Northamptonshire Police, 35
Northumberland, 123, 135
Northumbria
Newcastle-upon-Tyne, 135
Northumbria Police, 101, 111
Nottinghamshire, 4, 10, 14, 17, 18, 19, 20, 21, 22, 23, 24, 30, 41, 56, 57, 59, 62, 64, 85, 116, 117, 118, 123, 126, 133, 135, 136
Annesley colliery, 125
Ashfield, 133
Babbington colliery, 123

Index

Bevercotes Colliery,, 139
Cotgrave Colliery, 120
Creswell colliery, 123
Gedling colliery, 123
Harworth, 120
Harworth colliery, 92, 120, 135
Hucknall colliery, 120
Hucknall colliery, 116
Hucknall colliery, 134
Mansfield, 125, 139, 145, 150
Newstead colliery, 125
Ollerton, 84
Ollerton colliery, 84, 116, 117
Pye Colliery, 121
Retford, 136
Rufford colliery, 125
Rufford colliery, 126
Sherwood colliery, 125
Welbeck colliery, 126, 137
Worksop, 152
Nottinghamshire Police, 14, 17, 18, 20, 22, 41, 62, 98, 101, 111
Orgreave, 52, 53, 55, 85, 86, 93, 126, 127, 129
Picketing, 7, 10, 14, 22, 23, 26, 32, 41, 51, 55, 62, 69, 84, 85, 97, 100, 116, 117, 118, 119, 120, 121, 122, 123, 124, 125, 126, 127, 128, 129, 130, 131, 132, 133, 134, 137, 140, 141, 142, 143, 144, 145, 147, 148, 149, 150, 151
flying pickets, 31, 50, 53, 55, 84, 116
pickets. *See* Picketing
PNC. *See* Police National Computer
POFPU. *See* Public Order Forward Planning Unit
Police & Crime Commissioners, 47
Police Act 1964, vi, vii, 5, 6, 30, 62
Police Authorities, 29, 30, 63
Police Federation, 65, 95
Police National Computer, 12, 19
Police Regulations, 27, 65, 66, 81
Police Scotland, 6, 37
Police Service
 budget cuts, 81
 capability of, 59, 70, 79, 81
 cordial relations with striking miners, 51
 cost of policing the strike, 62, 63
 discrediting of, 50, 56, 70, 73, 82
 employment status, 81
 impact on families, 66, 67, 73
 letters of appreciation, 110
 misconduct, 50, 110, *See* Appendix 6B *passim.*

160

national, vii, 36
primary duty, vi, 29, 30, 55, 59, 110
public perception of, 66, 70, 79
welfare support, 67, 95
Police Support Unit, 7, 14, 17, 18, 19, 20, 22, 24, 26, 29, 30, 32, 43, 45, 53, 54, 57, 95, 96, 97, 99
  command of, 32, 33, 65, 95
  composition of, 7, 26, 99
  numbers of, 26, 54, 96
Politics. *See* Government
Prime Minister, 39, 57, 58, 63, 75
  Thatcher, Margaret, 2, 63
PSU. *See* Police Support Unit
Public Order
  tactic, 55
Public Order Forward Planning Unit, 4, 15, 20, 34, 42, 78, 79
  Tactical Operations Manual, 4, 42, 78
Public Order Training, 42, 78
  Regional Command Band Public Order Courses, 34
Public Relations, 36, 37, 38, 48, 51, 56, 66, 82
Riots, ix, 3, 6, 8, 11, 15, 42, 50, 78, 81, 82

preparation for, 3, 26, *See* Public Order Forward Planning Unit
Royal Commission, vi, 30
Saltley Depot, 53
Scab, 121, 150
Scotland, ii, iii, 4, 6, 7, 11, 12, 29, 37, 47, 53, 71, 78, 144, 146, 149
  Hunterston, 121
South Wales, 6, 15, 18, 27, 28, 41, 52, 56, 58, 86, 88, 118, 122, 131, 151
  Garw colliery, 136
  Glamorganshire, 6
  Llanwern, 52, 56
  miners allegiances, 57, 58
  Port Talbot, 52, 56, 86, 122, 123, 131, 151
South Wales Police, 15, 18, 27, 28, 41, 52, 98, 101, 111
South Yorkshire, 4, 28, 53, 54, 57, 58, 85, 122
  Barnsley, 116
  Cadley Hill colliery, 118
  Doncaster, 117, 121, 122, 130, 134, 141, 143
  Grimethorpe, 93
  Grimethorpe colliery, 119
  Hatfield Colliery, 141
  Houghton Main colliery, 116
  Kiverton Park colliery, 145
  Rotherham, 87, 128, 139, 140, 148

Index

Sheffield, 52, 53, 120
Silverwood colliery, 140
South Yorkshire Police, 28, 53, 99, 101, 112
Staffordshire, 24, 118, 135, 137, 151
   Hem Heath colliery, 93, 118, 119, 140
   Lea Hall colliery, 117
   Littleton colliery, 120
   Newcastle-under-Lyme, 122, 144
   Silverdale colliery, 118, 122, 124, 128
   Stoke-on-Trent, 118, 120, 123, 138, 140, 151
Staffordshire Police, 99, 101, 112
street disorders. *See* Riots
Strike Pay, 23, 50, 51, 69
Striking Miners, 10, 17, 18, 24, 48, 50, 51, 57, 58, 69, 73, 88, 89, 135, 139, 140, 146, 147, 149, 152
   death of, 84, 86
   impact on family, 51, 58, 67
   injured, 85
   returning to work, 56, 57, 58, 77, 88, 89
Suffolk Constabulary, 99
Surrey, ii
   Guildford, ii
Surrey Police, ii
Sussex, 57
   Brighton, 57, 87, 96

Conservative Party conference bombing, 57, 87, 96
Sussex Police, 99, 101
Thames Valley Police, 101, 112
Thatcher, Margaret. *See* Prime Minister
The Miners' Dispute. A Catalogue of Violence, 58, 70, 71, 72, 77, 114
Trades' Union, iv, v, 1, 2, 69
   congress, 89
   power of, v, 1
Tyne and Wear, 132
Violence, 22, 32, 41, 48, 50, 51, 55, 56, 57, 68, 71, 73, 85, 87, 97, 129, 142, *See* Appendix 7 *passim.*
   non-miners, 51, 58, 117
   police and miners, 18, 24, 48, 50, 55, 59, 117, 118, 119, 124, 125, 126, 129, 130, 131, 137, 138, 139, 145
   working and striking miners, 24, 48, 58, 59, 71, 72, 73, 117, 118, 120, 124, 125, 126, 134, 135, 136, 147, 151
Warwickshire, 24, 121, 139
   Birch Coppice colliery, 134
Warwickshire Police, 24, 99, 101, 112
West Yorkshire Police, 99, 101, 112, 131
Wiltshire Constabulary, 28

Winter of Discontent, 1
Wivenhoe Docks, 119
Working Miners, 22, 23, 24, 30, 37, 49, 50, 51, 56, 57, 58, 64, 69, 72, 73, 74, 77, 85, 115, 117, 118, 120, 125, 134, 135, 136, 141, 146, 147, 151
  impact on family, 58, 59, 67, 73, 77
  injuries, 72
  National Working Miners Committee. *See* National Working Miners Committee
  suicide of, 72, 121, 129
Wright, Peter, 54
Yorkshire, 57

The author today